RIFLES AND PISTOLS

JEREMY FLACK

PRC

Acknowledgements

I would like to acknowledge the help and encouragement received from the following people, in compiling this book: W.O. Ray Davies and Ken Murkin of the Royal Military College of Science at Shrivenham; Lt Col 'Tug' Wilson MBE and especially Major John Oldfield at the Infantry and Small Arms School Corps Weapon Museum, Warminster, Wilts. I would also like to thank my wife Julie and daughter Loretta who greatly assisted me.

This edition published in 1995 by the Promotional Reprint Company,
Deacon House, 65 Old Church Street, London SW3 5BS
exclusively for Booksales in New York, Coles in Canada and Chris Beckett Ltd. in New Zealand.

ISBN 1 85648 262 6

Printed and bound in China

CONTENTS

INTRODUCTION

Over the centuries, a tremendous variety of rifles and pistols have been developed. In the early days, these weapons required gunpowder, a material used in Chinese fireworks long before it was used in weapons. The date of the first instrument that combined gunpowder with a cannon and a projectile is unknown. However, a simple gun was known to be in existence from the early 14th century.

This book describes and illustrates the development of rifles and pistols from the basic simple matchlock through to the modern assault rifle. While compiling the data, a wide range of discrepancies were discovered regarding weight and dimensions. Some of this is due to the early methods of construction and the densities of the various woods used. The inclusion of ammunition and/or accessories such as tools, sights and bayonets, in the published weight was inconsistent. In this book, the weight and dimension listed is for the unloaded weapon and includes only those accessories actually shown in the illustration.

The effective range of a weapon is determined by numerous factors including the user's skill, the wind, and the ammunition quality. Therefore the given range of the rifles should only be taken as a nominal distance. Pistols have all been classified as short range weapons in this book, although some modern weapons have quite a long range.

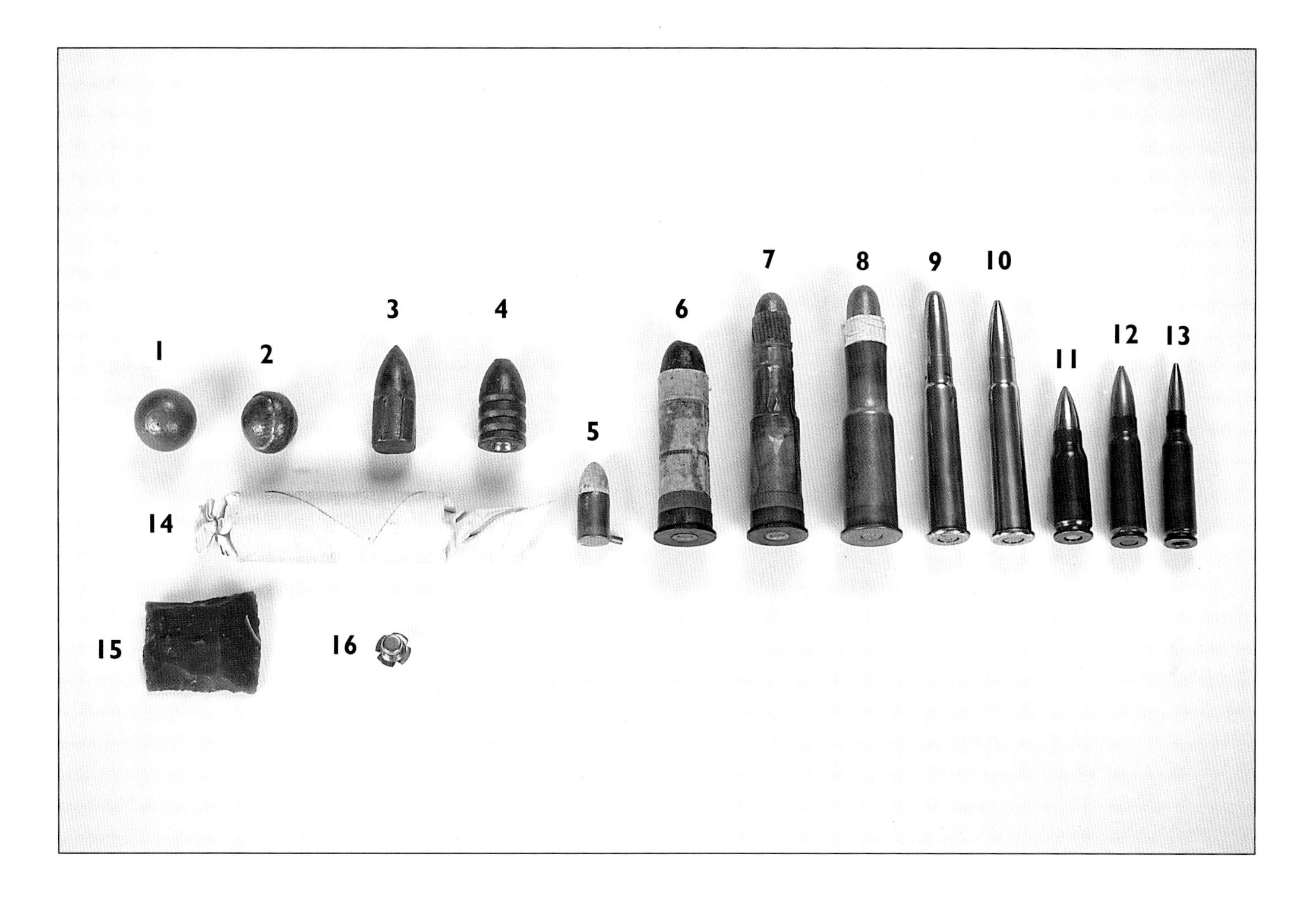

AMMUNITION: The shot or bullet has developed in design in parallel with the rifle and pistol.

1 Early musket smooth ball (7.25 in)
2 Double grooved ball (7.25 in) introduced for the Brunswick
3 Four grooved bullet (7.25 in) for the Jacob
4 Hollow bullet (5.77 in) of the Minie type rifles
5 Pin fire cartridge from a pistol
6 5.77 in Enfield Snider centre fire cartridge
7 4.5/5.77 in rolled brass cartridge for the Martini-Henry
8 4.5/5.77 in drawn brass cartridge for Martini-Henry
9 3.03 in Metford type cartridge with rounded bullet and
10 similar cartridge with a pointed bullet
11 7.92 mm German Kurz cartridge for the MP.44
12 Short 7.62 mm cartridge used mainly with Kalashnikov rifles
13 5.45 mm cartridge – the current Russian small calibre for AK-47
14 Powder cartridge containing the measured quantity of black powder
15 Piece of Iron Pyrities to provide the spark for flintlock weapons
16 Percussion cap which contained fulminate of mercury

EARLY DEVELOPMENT
1300–1800

The large early cannons soon led to small portable instruments which could be carried by one or two men. The earliest handguns typically comprised a tube closed at one end with a small hole drilled at that end. This was fitted onto a wooden shaft which could be dug into the ground enabling aim with one hand and igniting the powder with the other. This shaft would also absorb the recoil. While the noise and shock element was useful, the accuracy and effectiveness of this style of weapon left much to be desired.

The first major milestone was the matchlock at the turn of the 14th century. The term 'lock' referred to the method of igniting or firing the gunpowder. With the matchlock, the earlier loading principal was retained but some of the powder was placed in a priming pan and ignited by a slow match on one end of a lever or 'trigger'. This enabled a controlled and, for the first time, a real aim at the target. This simple weapon was cheap to produce and remained in widespread use well after more effective types became available. They were still in use by the tribesmen of India on the North-West Frontier in the 1930s.

Development of the rifle through the musket and that of the pistol followed roughly hand in hand. However, the pistol never gained the confidence of the rifle due to the inaccuracy of its short barrel. As a result, its effective range was limited to that of not much greater than a sword. Being unreliable and, at that period, the time to reload too great, the pistol had little success until the arrival of the revolver. Even then, the numbers have never matched those of the rifle with its accuracy at distance. What the pistol did manage to provide was a convenient means of defence for the close encounter for which the rifle was too cumbersome. As a result the mass produced military pistol or revolver was and is more likely to be issued to officers, guards and special forces.

The matchlock brought about the beginning of the musket as a portable means of firing a shot. However, it was also very weather dependent and reloading remained time consuming. The slow match could not be lit or was put out in rain. Even if it remained alight, the powder in the pan would not ignite once it became damp. The problem of the wet pan was relatively easy to resolve by moving it to the side and fitting a lid. This also enabled the maintaining of a loaded weapon in readiness. The slow match problem was not so easy to resolve.

One of the main problems of the matchlock musket was the time to reload. First the slow match had to be removed and then the priming powder would be placed in the pan and closed off. Next a measured amount of powder would be poured into the barrel of the musket followed by the shot. These were then rammed down, the slow match returned and blown to make it glow. The weapon was then ready to fire.

Various modifications were applied to the matchlock principle in order to improve its efficiency and accuracy. These included the cocking button lock, pressure lock and the snap lock. In addition other refinements began to be investigated with varying degrees of success, such as rifling, addition of sights and even early attempts at breech-loading. The latter were not very successful due to the lack of gas seal. However, further experiments were made with various forms of quick loading such as a succession of shots loaded down the same barrel. The latter would be fired by individual fore holes but tended to leak fire back past the shot to fire the next shot early or even blow up the barrel. Even multi-barrel arrangements were tried. These weapons were changing the style of battles as the attacks by cavalry or infantry could be checked by volleys of the inaccurate matchlock muskets.

The wheel lock was the next major advance when it was introduced in the early 16th century. This clockwork driven mechanism worked in a similar fashion to the modern flint lighter, showering the primer with sparks. This would ignite the priming powder which then ignited the main charge.

Due to its cost, the wheel lock was initially only used by wealthy sportsmen and officers and was often highly decorated. When it eventually was issued in limited numbers to the military, the wheel lock pistol provided the first practical firearm for those on horseback and at the same time making practicable a hand weapon.

The wheel lock was, however, very unreliable. The spring would break or the mechanism would jam or the pyrites could shatter. The original problem of reloading time still remained.

Various potential solutions evolved ranging from multi-barrel weapons through to superimposed charges. Several breech-loading, magazine-fed wheel and flint locks were made during the 17th century.

The introduction of the cartridge in about 1700 provided a major improvement in the reloading time. It no longer became necessary to measure the quantity of powder as this had already been done and was sealed in the paper tube. All the musketeer had to do was to tear the tube and pour the contents into the barrel. The shot was pushed into the barrel followed by the paper and rammed home.

Archers had previously discovered that setting the feathers on an arrow at an angle to impart a spin led to greater accuracy. This idea was applied to firearms and further developed with anything from 2 to 34 grooves within the barrel.

The tighter fit required for rifling to impart spin could be effected by patching the wrapping of the bullet in tallow soaked linen or buckskin. This also reduced the need for a mallet to force the bullet down onto the rifling. However, loading a rifle as opposed to a smooth bore musket continued to be a relatively slow process. In attempts to speed up the rate of fire of rifles, there was intensive development of the breech loader during the 18th century.

The next main firing system that was developed was the flintlock although the snaphaunce and miquelet provided an earlier and more basic similar form. The first true flintlock emerged in the early 17th century. Here the steel and pan are combined into a single 'L' shaped item. In addition, a means of locking the hammer at half cock with a catch or 'dog' eliminated the possibility of an accidental firing. To fire the musket or rifle, the hammer was simply drawn back to fully cocked position and the trigger pulled, the cock containing the flint would strike the steel, simultaneously exposing the pan and showering the priming powder with sparks.

The widespread success of the flintlock arrangement was due to its simplicity and reliability of the mechanism, ease of manufacture and therefore cost. The mechanism even had wider use for igniting cannons and rockets as well as tinder boxes in the home. It was, however, by modern standards, not very reliable in causing the weapon to actually fire.

The smooth bore flintlock muskets remained much the same from the late 17th century through to the first half of the 19th century. However, reloading remained relatively slow and aim inaccurate. These weapons depended on regular volleys from disciplined troops in square or line formation for effect. The musket was not accurate since, in order to facilitate rapid loading, the ball was substantially smaller than the bore.

In 1776, an Englishman by the name of Captain Ferguson developed a breech loader which used a screw plug that enabled the shot to be dropped in. The shot would roll forward to the beginning of the rifling enabling the powder to be poured in. The cavity was calculated to ensure that the correct amount of powder was used. The plug was screwed back, primed and fired. This followed an existing French design but Ferguson's development managed to unscrew and rescrew the plug with a single turn compared with the existing system that required many turns. Ferguson successfully demonstrated his idea but it was never adopted. One hundred were built for an experimental rifle unit to fight the American colonials but the idea did not catch on.

As with the matchlock and wheel lock rifles and pistols, various forms of breech arrangements were designed and many were built although few had success.

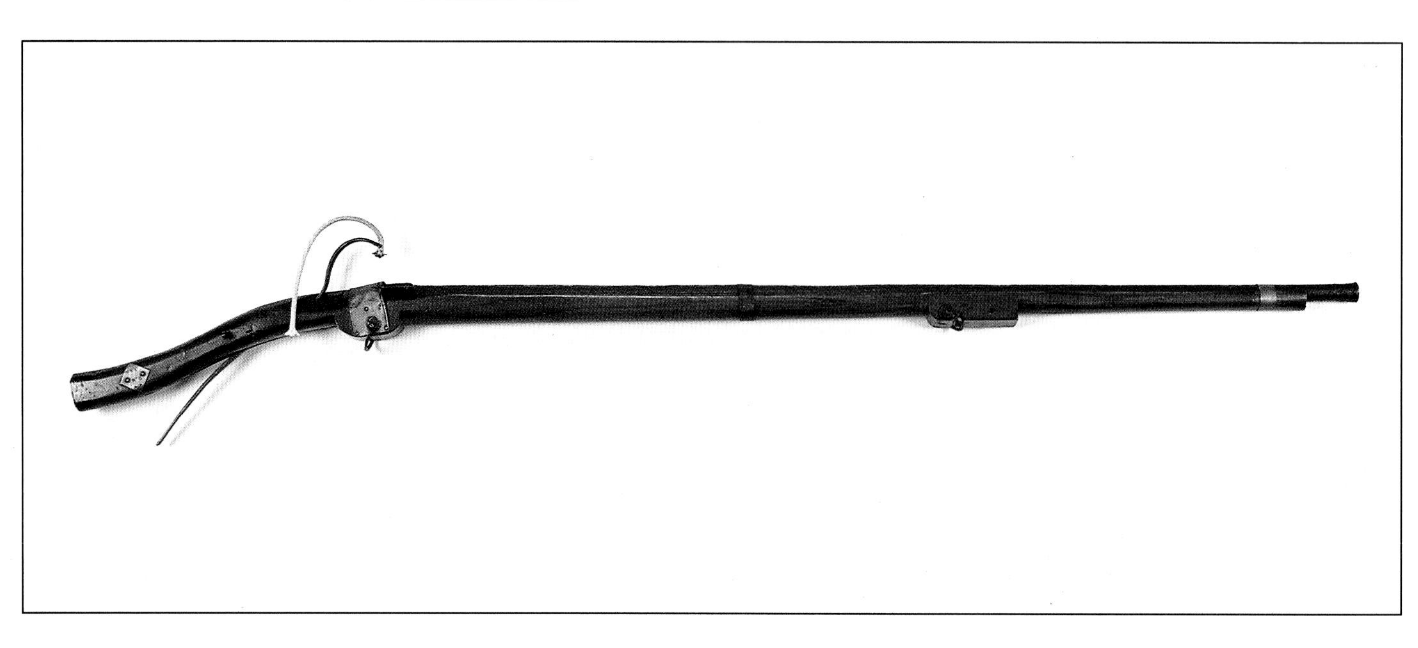

TYPE:	**0.436 IN MATCHLOCK MUSKET**
MANUFACTURER:	not known
DATE IN USE:	15th century
COUNTRY OF MANUFACTURE:	India
OPERATION:	muzzle loading, matchlock
LENGTH:	59 in/1,499 mm
WEIGHT:	9 lb/4.09 kg
EFFECTIVE RANGE:	109 yd/100 m

This very crude handmade musket uses the earliest known type of lock of the 15th century. It is thought to be Indian and may have still been in use in the late 19th or early 20th century.

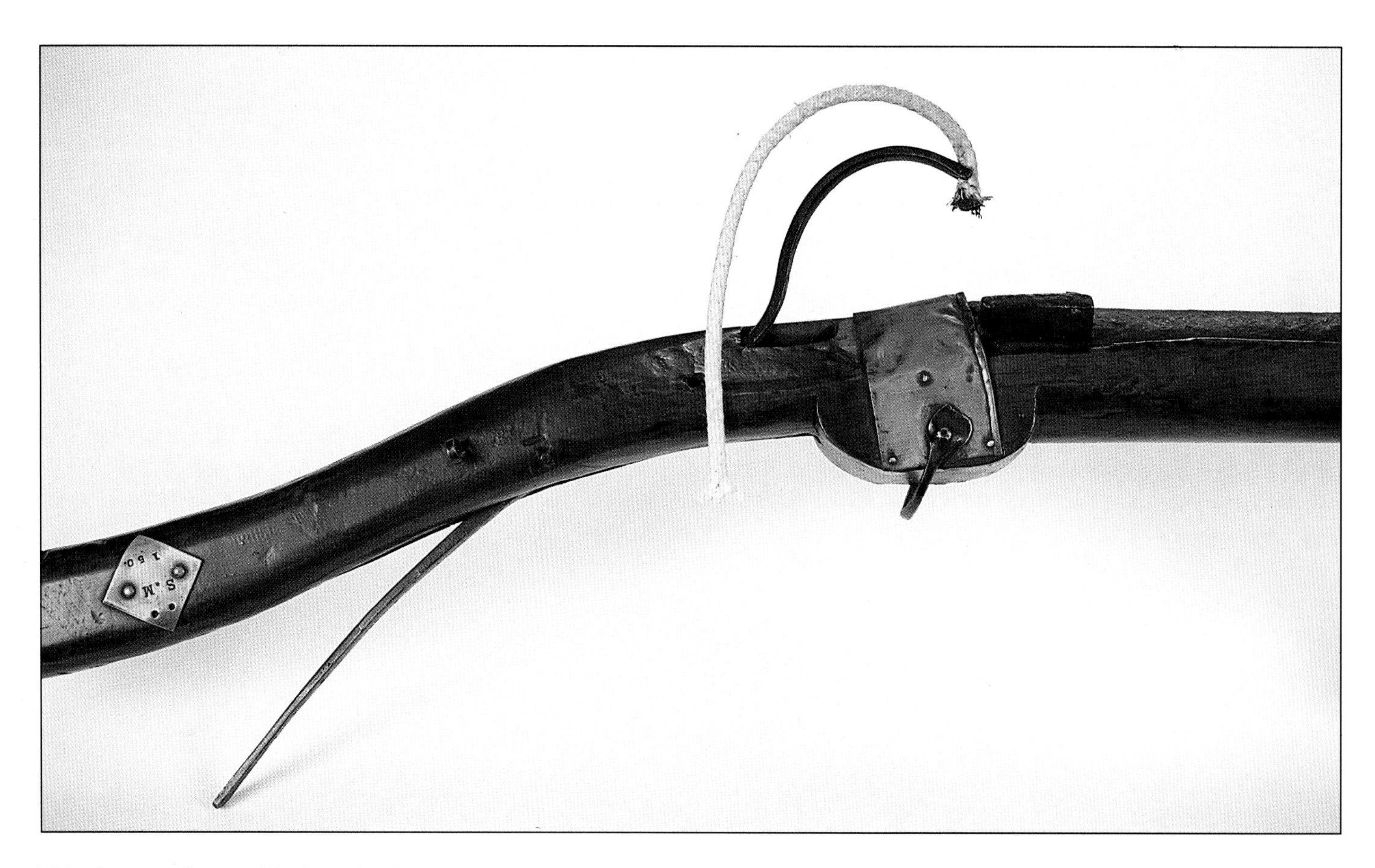

This close up of a matchlock mechanism shows the simple way of holding the slow match. The action of squeezing the lever lowers it onto the priming charge causing it to ignite and then fire the main charge.

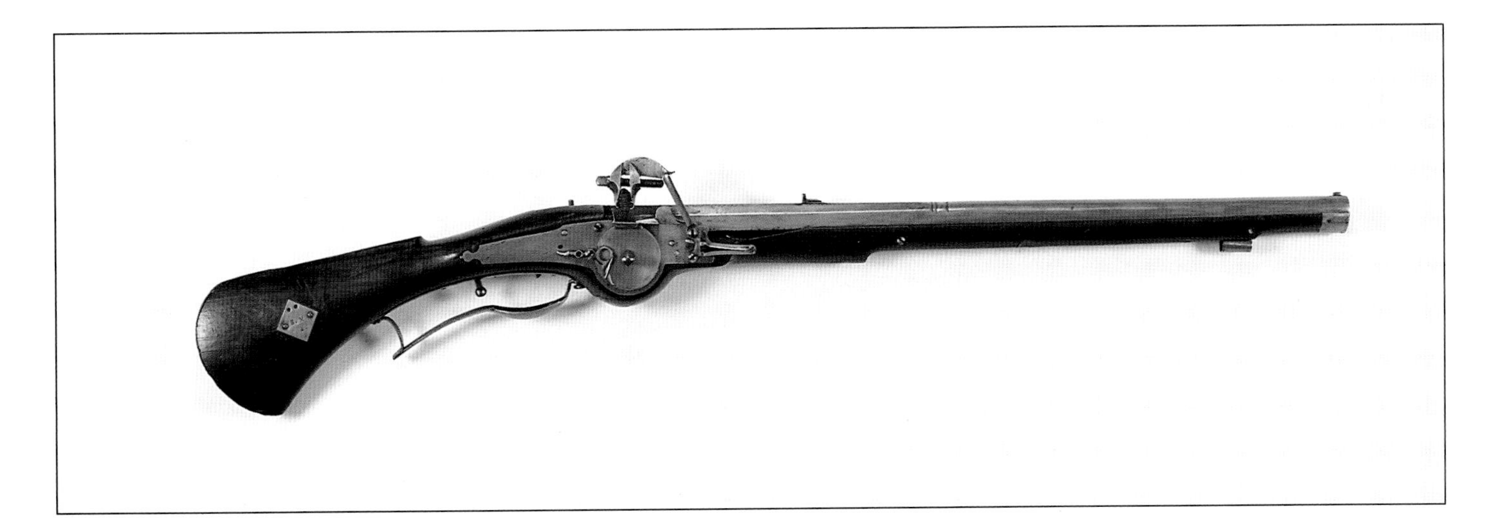

TYPE:	**0.75 IN WHEEL-LOCK CAVALRY CARBINE**
MANUFACTURER:	not known
DATE IN USE:	16th century
COUNTRY OF MANUFACTURE:	Netherlands
OPERATION:	muzzle loading, wheel lock
LENGTH:	37.25 in/945 mm
WEIGHT:	6.75 lb/3.06 kg
EFFECTIVE RANGE:	82 yd/75 m

After the matchlock, the next major advance in firing mechanism design was the invention of the wheel lock during the early 16th century. This system replaced the slow match with a clockwork powered serrated steel wheel which worked in a similar fashion to the modern flint lighter.

In addition to its use on rifles and muskets, the wheel lock enabled the production of the first practical handgun but because of its cost and the fragile nature of the lock which required skilful repairs, it was never widely used by the military.

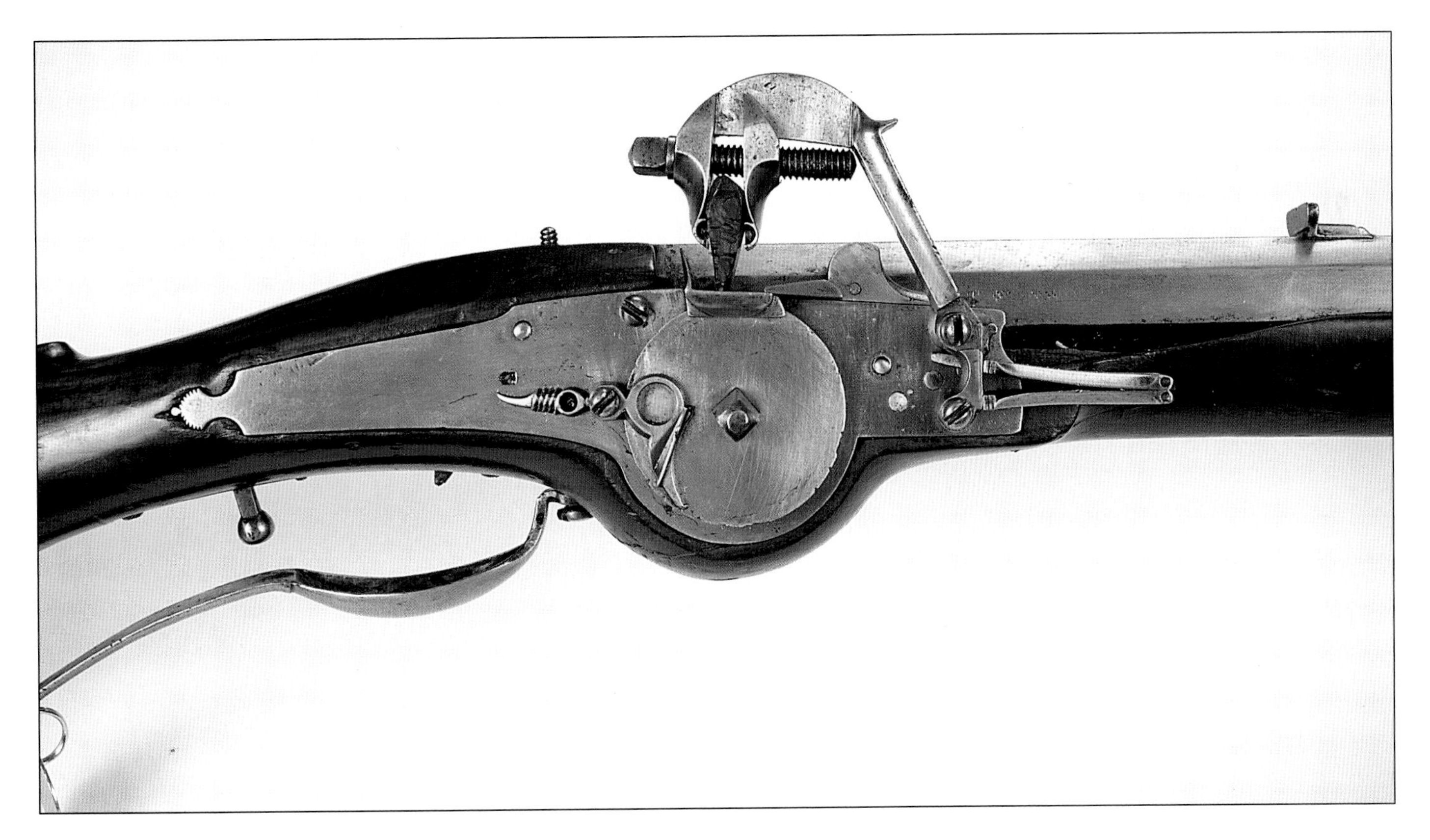

The weapon was loaded in the same way as the matchlock but instead of checking the state of the slow match, the pan cover would be opened and the trigger pulled. This would cause the wheel to revolve, rubbing against a piece of iron pyrites or flint and showering the pan with sparks. This ignited the primer which set off the main charge.

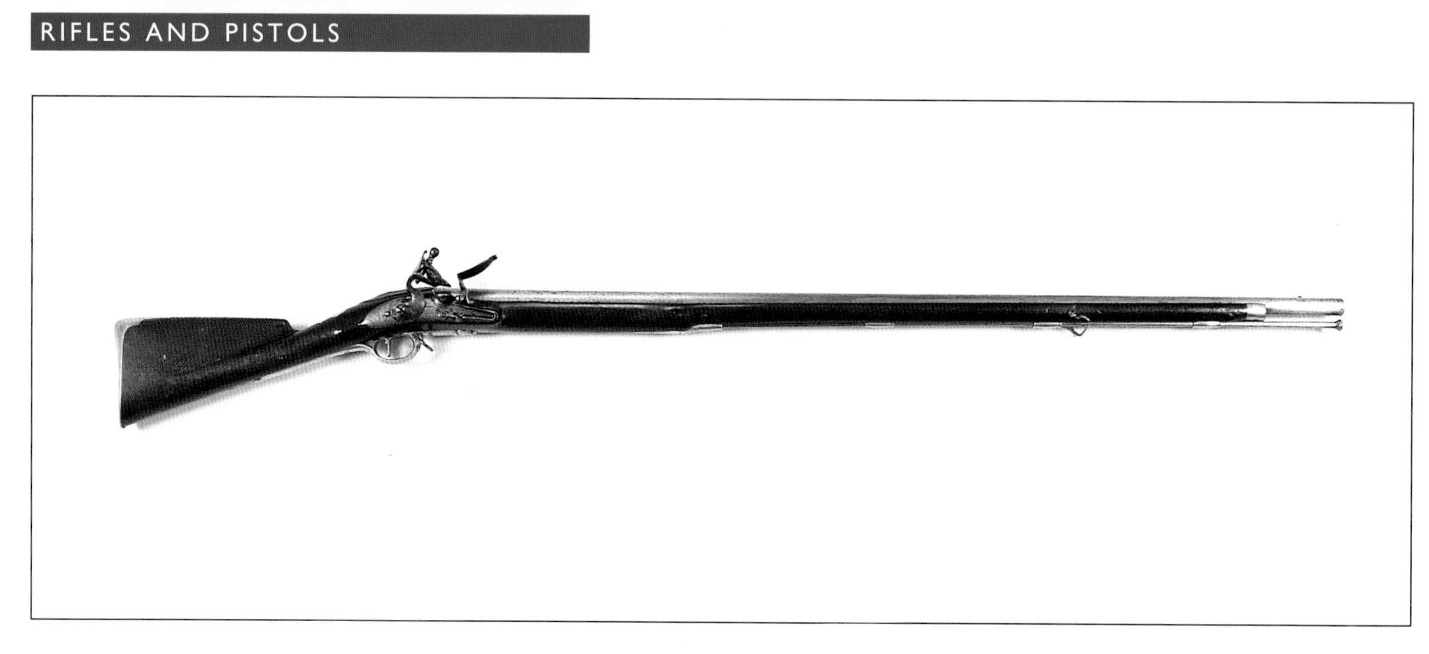

TYPE:	**10 BORE BROWN BESS (EARLY)**
MANUFACTURER:	E Cookes
DATE IN USE:	1700
COUNTRY OF MANUFACTURE:	UK
OPERATION:	muzzle loading, flintlock
LENGTH:	47 in/1,193 mm
WEIGHT:	8.5 lb/3.32 kg
EFFECTIVE RANGE:	82 yd/75 m

The Brown Bess was typical of the smooth bore muskets of its day. The cartridge consisted of the paper cylinder with 6 to 8 drams of powder. The end would be bitten off, a small amount of powder poured into the open pan then closed. The rest of the powder would be poured into the barrel and the ball together with the paper rammed home. A trained soldier could manage three to four rounds per minute.

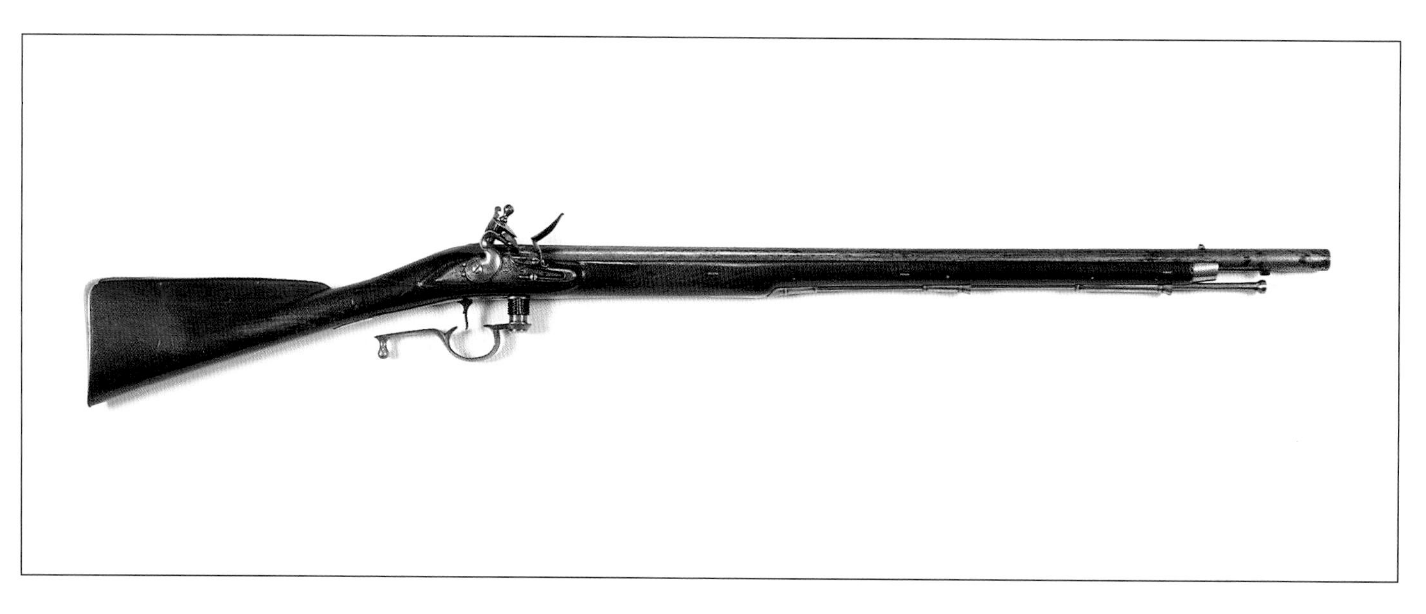

TYPE:	**.5 IN FERGUSON RIFLE**
MANUFACTURER:	Durs Egg
DATE IN USE:	1776
COUNTRY OF MANUFACTURE:	UK
OPERATION:	breech-loading, flintlock
LENGTH:	61 in/1,549 mm
WEIGHT:	11 lb/4.99 kg
EFFECTIVE RANGE:	273yd/250 m

The Ferguson rifle was fitted with breech-loading. The trigger guard was given a single turn, a plug lowered allowing the ball and then powder to be loaded into the hole on the top. The trigger guard was turned back which raised the plug and forced out surplus powder. After priming, the rifle was then ready to fire. The weapon could be fired six times in one minute. This particular Durs Egg Ferguson is rifled with seven grooves.

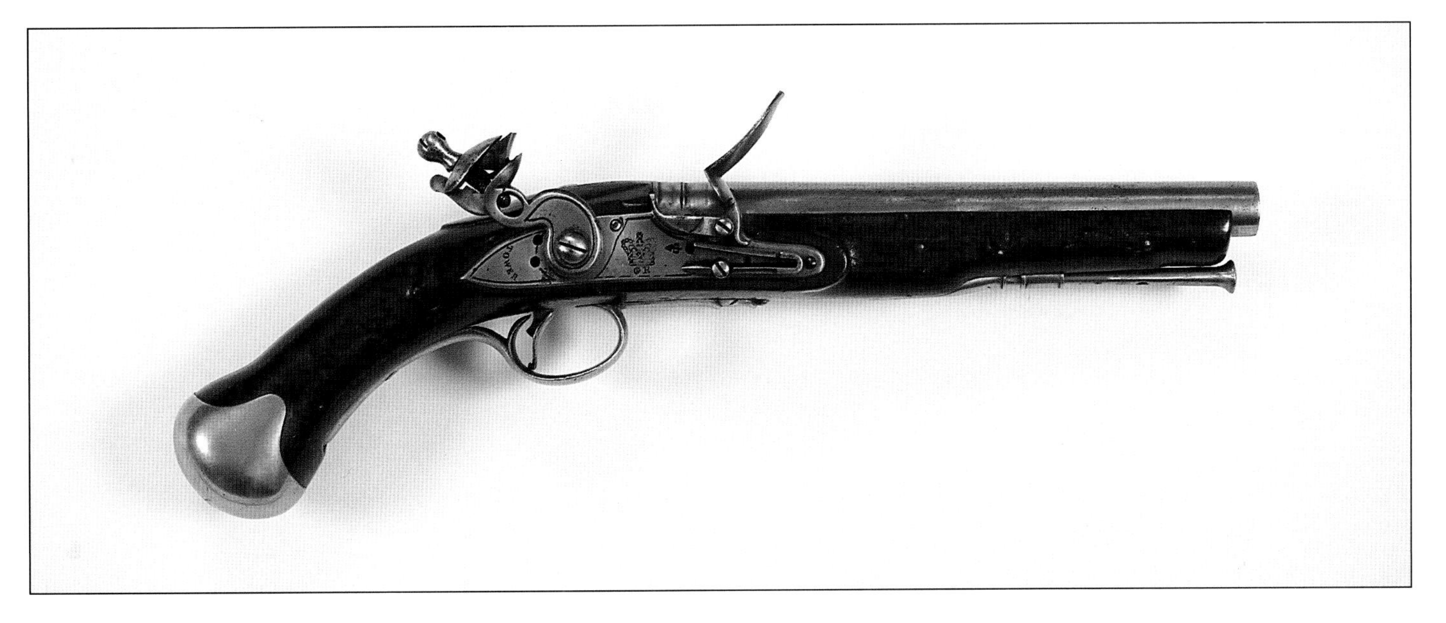

TYPE:	**0.57 IN SEA-SERVICE FLINTLOCK PISTOL**
MANUFACTURER:	Tower
DATE IN USE:	1790
COUNTRY OF MANUFACTURE:	UK
OPERATION:	muzzle loading, flintlock
LENGTH:	16 in/406 mm
WEIGHT:	3 lb/1.36 kg
EFFECTIVE RANGE:	close quarters

The flintlock was widely used for military pistols. In good conditions it would work four times out of five.

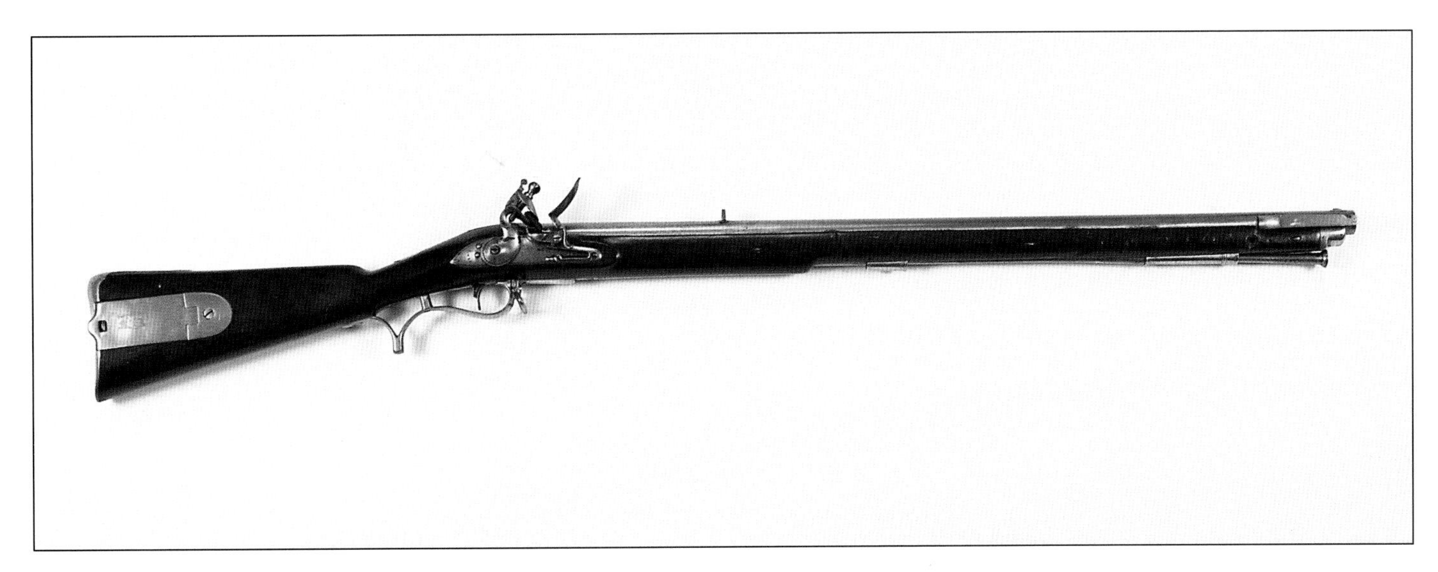

TYPE:	**.65 IN BAKER RIFLE**
MANUFACTURER:	Tower
DATE IN USE:	1800
COUNTRY OF MANUFACTURE:	UK
OPERATION:	muzzle loading, flintlock
LENGTH:	45.9 in/1,166 mm
WEIGHT:	8 lb/3.63 kg
EFFECTIVE RANGE:	164 yd/150 m

From 1800 the new and experimental British Rifle Corps was issued with this rifle. Greased pieces of leather or cloth were stored in the brass box fitted in the butt. Once the powder was poured into the muzzle, a piece of this was placed over the end of the barrel and a shot put on top before being rammed home.

The Baker was probably the first rifle to be issued in quantity. This weapon was a compromise between ease of loading and the imparting of spin to increase accuracy. As a result, the barrel had a one quarter turn in the 30 in length. Although slower to load – three shots in two minutes – it could be reasonably expected to hit a man at 100 m and good shots might be allowed to practise up to 200 m. The Baker rifle was issued to British Rifle Regiments.

THE CENTURY OF INNOVATIONS
1801–1900

By the beginning of the 19th century new developments in the ammunition field were emerging. The possibilities of fulminates had interested several experimenters in the quest for speed and reliability of fire. A parish priest of Belhelvie in Scotland, Alexander Forsyth, might seem an unusual munition expert to us today. However, the Rev Forsyth was interested in shooting game and was trying to resolve the problem of the flash of the priming powder alerting the game before the main charge fired. In 1805, after much experimenting, he devised a method whereby a little 'scent bottle' like container would deposit a small amount of fulminate in the touch hole, the hammer would strike it and the resulting explosion set off the main charge.

The Rev Forsyth took his idea to the Master General of the Ordnance and was allowed to develop it further. However, a subsequent change in the Master resulted in a reversal of interest. He patented his 'scent bottle' lock and, after setting up a commercial partnership, Forsyth returned to his parish. When the patent ran out various attempts were made by others to simplify the process.

Eventually, an effective and manageable system in the form of the percussion cap evolved. Using a copper cap containing some fulminate, the percussion cap was placed over a hollow nipple. When struck by the hammer it would immediately fire the main charge. As this system became more widely accepted, large numbers of conversions of flint lock to percussion cap resulted.

The British Army took interest and a trial was instigated. Six flint lock muskets and six percussion cap muskets were to fire 6,000 rounds. The results were quite staggering. The flint locks had 922 misfires (averaging one in six and a half) while the percussion had only 136 (one in 166). The flint scored 3,690 hits while the percussion had 4,047. It took 32 minutes and 31 seconds for the flint lock to fire 100 shots and 30 minutes 24 seconds for the percussion. On receiving the results the Board of Ordnance decided to re-equip the whole Army with percussion weapons. This was a huge undertaking and would largely be achieved by converting the old flint locks. Unfortunately, thousands were destroyed in a huge fire at the Tower of London. However, this resulted in the purchase of the new Pattern 1842 although some Pattern 1839 were acquired as a stopgap.

Designs continued to be developed, including several laminating the fulminate in paper, resulting in caps which were similar to those used in modern toy guns. Some well in advance of their time barely surfaced and were overlooked. In 1812, a Swiss man named Pauly developed a breech-loading sports gun with a cartridge which consisted of a reusable brass case with priming cap, paper body containing the main charge and the shot on the top. This cartridge was centre fired but despite numerous demonstrations, military interest was not forthcoming and it was another 50 years before a similar system was reinvented.

In the meantime, probably the first successful breech-loading rifle had been patented in 1811 – the Hall Rifle. This American flint lock rifle comprised a chamber which was released by pressing down on a short lever. This enabled the charge to be inserted, snapped closed, primed and fired.

The needle and pin fire were the next advances in ignition. Johann Nikolaus Dreyse had been a lockmaker for Pauly and returned to Prussia where he set up a percussion cap factory. By taking Pauly's firing pin system, Dreyse located the percussion fulminate in the hollowed out base of the lead bullet. When the trigger was pulled, the needle was forced through the base of the cartridge and the powder and struck the fulminate which ignited the powder. The main disadvantage of the needle fire was the fragility of the pin. The early experiments were initially conducted with a muzzle loader but he invented a breech-loading system in 1837. This was to lead the way for subsequent bolt-action rifles despite snags with the gas seal between breech and lock.

The hand rotated pepper-box pistol first appeared in the 1820s as a solution to the problem of quick reloading. This was achieved by mounting a number of barrels together. Later, still using the percussion cap or pin fire to fire the barrels, these were mechanically rotated when the hammer was cocked. Amongst the first to build such pistols were the American, Ethan Allan, in 1837 and the Belgian, Mariette. The pepper-box was a cumbersome pistol being inherently heavy and badly balanced.

Invention of the pin fire cartridge was credited to the Frenchman, Lefaucheux, in 1835, although this was a development of Houiller's idea . The cartridge was roughly similar to that of the needle fire except that the percussion cap was set at right angles to the brass base with a pin projecting from the cap and out of the side of the case. When the trigger was squeezed, the hammer released and the pin was struck and driven into the cap, causing the fulminate to explode and the main charge to ignite.

The pin fire was used by both sides during the American Civil War and was widely used for sporting weapons. Its principal disadvantage was the fragility of the pin which could be easily damaged, coupled with the inherent instability of the cartridge which could be fired by accidental pressure.

In 1836 the Brunswick rifle was adopted by the British Army for rifle regiments. Although successful in trials it was deemed a failure in the field. The barrel had twin grooves and fired a belted ball. There were two problems with this system. The ball being belted was susceptible to cross winds and the tightness of fit required considerable force to load.

Colonel Jacob conducted experiments and discovered that four grooves gave a much better result with a bullet shaped projectile. It was moulded with four lugs to fit the grooves. The suggestion to modify the Brunswick was rebuffed but Jacob continued with his experiments. Although not officially adopted, rifles to his design were used by the Indian Army and a regiment was formed and equipped with his design of double barrelled rifle at Jacob's own expense.

First patented in England in 1835, Samuel Colt designed a pistol which had a revolving cylinder which enabled five shots to be fired in quick succession. It followed the conventional form of loading in that the powder and ball had to be loaded from the front of the chamber and used percussion caps for igniting. The patents were so comprehensive that they precluded manufacture of virtually anything looking like a revolver until 1850. Colt hotly confronted any infringement with legal action. Colt found difficulty in penetrating the market dominated by the pepper-box and his first factory closed in 1843. Fortunately for Colt, several revolvers were seen by the Texas Rangers and when the Mexican War broke out they persuaded the government that this weapon was needed.

When word got through to Samuel Colt from Colonel Walker, production quickly followed with the Colt Walker. This was to become the first revolver to be issued to any army in the world. A range of revolvers soon emerged including the .36 Colt Navy in 1857 and the .44 Army in 1860.

At the same time, Colt was producing a repeating rifle of which the mechanism closely resembled that of the revolvers. A series of refinements over the following years saw the adoption in limited numbers of the Colt Repeating Rifle Model 1855 by the military.

The Dreyse bolt action rifle was tested by the Prussians in 1841 and adopted in 1848 due to its far superior rate of fire over the muzzle loading percussion rifles. This system was proved with the ease with which Prussia defeated Denmark and Austria in the mid 1860s. At this time France was adopting an improved needlefire system in the Chassepot. However, it was not until 1866 that the British began converting their muzzle loading rifle to breech loading.

In 1848, Christian Sharp patented his breech-loading mechanism that used the percussion cap as the means to fire the main charge. This patent led to numerous dropping block actions over a period of nearly 100 years.

The Sharps rifle was used extensively during the American Civil War. Other designs included the .52 Smith and another by Burnside resulted in orders for some 30,000 followed by 50,000 rifles together with some 13,000,000 and then nearly 22,000,000 special cartridges.

Jennings' toggle locked breech represented a further stepping stone for a number of new actions. These included the Winchester and Volcanic rifles, Maxim and Vickers machine guns and the Borchardt pistol which led to the Luger.

While the rifled barrel was to increase the accuracy, the main problem lay in the necessary tight fit required to stop the propellant gas escaping past the bullet. The answer came with the Minié which was used by the British Army from 1851. This heavily lubricated bullet was dropped down the barrel in the same way as the old musket ball. The secret of the idea was that the bullet was partially hollow and the charge exploding would force a heavy plug into the bullet which would swell the bullet sufficiently to expand it onto the rifling. Such was the accuracy that could now be achieved that the rifle was sighted at 820 m and at least one shot in seven would hit a target six feet by three at that range. At 460–730 m the hits increased to two out of five. The Enfield cartridge paper was waterproofed by being dipped in tallow (animal fat) and is said to have played a role in causing the Indian Mutiny. In the handling of forbidden animal products the Indian soldier believed that his religion was being defiled. The result was a mutiny which took two years to put down.

In 1851 an English Deane-Adams revolver was patented and offered strong competition to Colt. The Deane-Adams comprised a solid frame and was a much stronger design than the Colt. It was also double-action in that the pull on the trigger turned the cylinder, cocked and dropped the hammer. Unfortunately for Deane-Adams, Colt had utilised mass production techniques and was able to offer a cheaper weapon.

Deane-Adams fought back by designing the mechanism of his next revolver to be single and double-action. This combined the advantages of the faster firing double-action with the greater accuracy of the single-action.

Up to this point, the pistol mechanism had developed hand-in-hand with the musket or rifle. The single shot pistol had never really caught on as a military infantry weapon as it was virtually useless once fired. The multiple barrel and pepper-pot pistols did little to change this. However Colt's revolvers brought about a change in attitudes.

The Minié was replaced by the Pattern 1853 Enfield Rifle which had a .577 inch calibre, much smaller than the .702 inch of the 1851 model. These rifles came in a number of variations. The sergeant's rifle was 3 inches shorter than standard while the cavalry were equipped with even shorter carbines. The loading was still via the muzzle which remained a tight fit but this time the cartridges were encased in greased paper and the bullet oiled to reduce friction, which proved effective.

In 1854 a breech-loader by James Leech was tested by Woolwich and as a result an order was placed for the British Army. Further interest in breech-loaders produced further trials. This time it was carbines by the British men, Terry and Westley Richards and Americans, Sharps and Greene. When the Greene was dropped, orders were placed for various quantities of the different carbines over the following few years.

The emergence of Smith & Wesson with .22 inch metal rim fire cartridges brought about a compact revolver which was light and easy to load. This became possible through the acquisition of a patent for bored through cylinders. As a result they soon became popular in the USA. Meanwhile in Continental Europe the introduction of the pin fire revolver was led by Lefaucheux.

The American and European revolvers followed two separate features. The Americans favoured the solid frame, while the Europeans prefered the hinged frame, the main exception being the Smith and Wesson.

Spencer's repeating rifle was first rebuffed by all the ordnance officers that he saw at the War Office at Washington. This was during the early days of the Civil War when everybody was trying to cope with their job in hand and not looking at hopefuls with their time-wasting inventions.

Totally disillusioned, Spencer was giving up but stopped on his way out to speak to the doorman. On hearing the story and being given a demonstration of the gun with dummy ammunition, the doorman suggested that Spencer returned when the doorman finished work and he would arrange for someone to see him.

This person turned out to be President Lincoln who watched Spencer demonstrate his rifle. Impressed, he tried the rifle himself and this resulted in Government orders for over 100,000 Spencer rifles by the time the war finished.

By 1860, obturation emerged as a means of sealing the metal cartridge. This provided a solution to the problems of the poor gas seal for the breech-loading rifle and the pistols. Colonel Boxer was credited with producing a coiled brass cartridge. The primer Boxer designed was simple and highly effective to the extent that it is still used today in the USA. It is made up of a small metal cup which contains the priming mixture and an anvil comprising a small pointed piece embedded in the primer. This was contained within the base of the cartridge. When the hammer hit the base of the cartridge it was compacted against the anvil and the friction ignited the primer and fired the main charge.

In 1862 the Henry repeater became available from Winchester. Although virtually ignored by the military, many individuals purchased the rifle during the American Civil War. Such was the reliability and repeating firepower of the Winchester rifles that production of the Model 1866 had reached 170,000 by 1898.

In 1865, Metford, a British consulting engineer, produced a design for rifling that was to become the world standard. Instead of a deep groove which rapidly fouled when using black powder, Metford's design was for shallow grooves in which the grooves and the lands were slightly rounded. This dramatically reduced the fouling as well as bullet deformation and was widely considered as superior to previous designs. While this worked well with black powder, it was found that the later introduction to cordite propellant had a corrosive effect and required a return to deeper rifling.

In 1866 work started to convert the large stocks of Enfield rifles to breech-loaders. This was achieved by the fitting of the American Snider breech block although this was just a temporary arrangement. In the meantime trials continued with some 120 rifles and 49 types of cartridge to determine the weapon for the future British Army. On completion, all of those tested were rejected and the committee re-sat the following year with a new brief.

Also in 1866, the design of the Remington rolling block was being completed and production commenced the following year with deliveries to the US and numerous other countries. Somewhere in the region of 1,000,000 rolling block rifles and carbines were built.

Peabody marketed a .50 inch calibre rifle with a falling block and was successful in generating orders from around Europe. The Swiss were impressed with this design and ordered 15,000 in 1867. These were subsequently given to a master mechanic for modification. Frederich von Martini fitted a leverage arrangement that automatically cocked the hammer as the action was opened. A further modification removed the old flintlock type hammer and replaced this with an internal hammer.

The original Peabody design was adopted and modified by a large number of arms manufacturers to the extent that nearly all pivoting breech block designs were based on the Peabody.

In 1867 the British committee decided on a new service rifle. Initially this was to incorporate the Martini action together with the Henry barrel. The action was simple and reliable and as a result was in service well into the 20th century especially with colonial forces and up to 1939 with the British Home Guard.

In most of Europe, bolt action rifles were increasingly recognised as the way ahead. Unfortunately a premature discharge with an early bolt rifle meant that the British virtually ruled them out.

About this time various forms of magazine were being developed including tubular with ammunition stored below the barrel. In 1879, James Lee patented a bolt action rifle fitted with a box magazine. This was to have a great influence on the development of future service rifles through to the end of World War One.

During the 1880s, trials were conducted by a number of countries to establish a greater velocity and thus a flatter trajectory of ammunition, in order to ensure that the bullet remained effective for as long as possible across the battlefield. Ideally it should not rise above head height and would thus reduce the error in judgement of distance. It was found that this was best achieved by reducing the calibre and lengthening the bullet.

While these were easily achievable the bullet was unstable and the only way of improving this was to increase the twist of the rifling. However, the lead bullet was too soft and invariably became stripped or distorted. A Swiss man by the name of Major Rubin strengthened his bullets with a layer of copper.

The revolver was reaching the end of its development, although it still remains popular today. However, the pistol was entering a new era. The power of the recoil could be harnessed to assist in the reloading of the weapon. This directly followed from Hiram Maxim's construction of the recoil operated machine gun.

The Borchardt Self-Loading Pistol was an early attempt to harness this force, but it was heavy and quite a clumsy weapon. However, it was later modified by Georg Luger to become the famous Luger Pistol. Peter Paul Mauser was famous for his rifles but his Model 1896 pistol proved to be a well built and effective weapon. It had a wooden holster which could be clipped onto the stock, converting it to a carbine. It was sighted to 1,094 yd (1,000 m) and it was this pistol that Winston Churchill carried in Sudan in 1898.

The introduction of the slow but reliable French Lebel rifle with a tube magazine resulted in the Germans adopting the Gewehr 88 in 1888. This rifle was fitted with a box magazine and loaded with cartridges filled with smokeless powder.

At the same time, the British had tested a variety of magazine types including tube and the Lee box type. In the end the Lee box magazine and bolt was selected together with Metford rifling and .303 calibre cartridge. This was to become known as the Lee-Metford Magazine Rifle Mark I. It was still several years before the US made a similar move to a magazine rifle.

Experiments had been conducted for some time to reduce the effect of the smoke produced by the black powder which not only gave away the firing positions, but could also obscure the target. In the UK in 1891 a new cartridge was introduced powered by cordite. Not only was this smokeless but it left little fouling, was extremely reliable and safe to handle. It was found that the very high combustion temperature of the cordite created excessive wear of the barrel and resulted in changing the rifling from the shallow Metford to a deeper square cut developed at Enfield. At the same time, a number of Martini-Henry rifles and carbines were modified to fire this new ammunition.

Having bought a quantity of the short-lived Krag-Jorgensen rifles, the Springfield Armoury began to produce a .30 inch calibre version of the Mauser Gewehr 98. This followed trials on captured German-made Spanish examples. Initially these were little better than the Krag but following various small alterations the Model 1906 proved to be satisfactory.

During the 19th century the development of rifles, their range, lethality and finally rapid rate of fire almost always outpaced the ability of both senior officers and soldiers to appreciate the tactical and logistical significance of these developments.

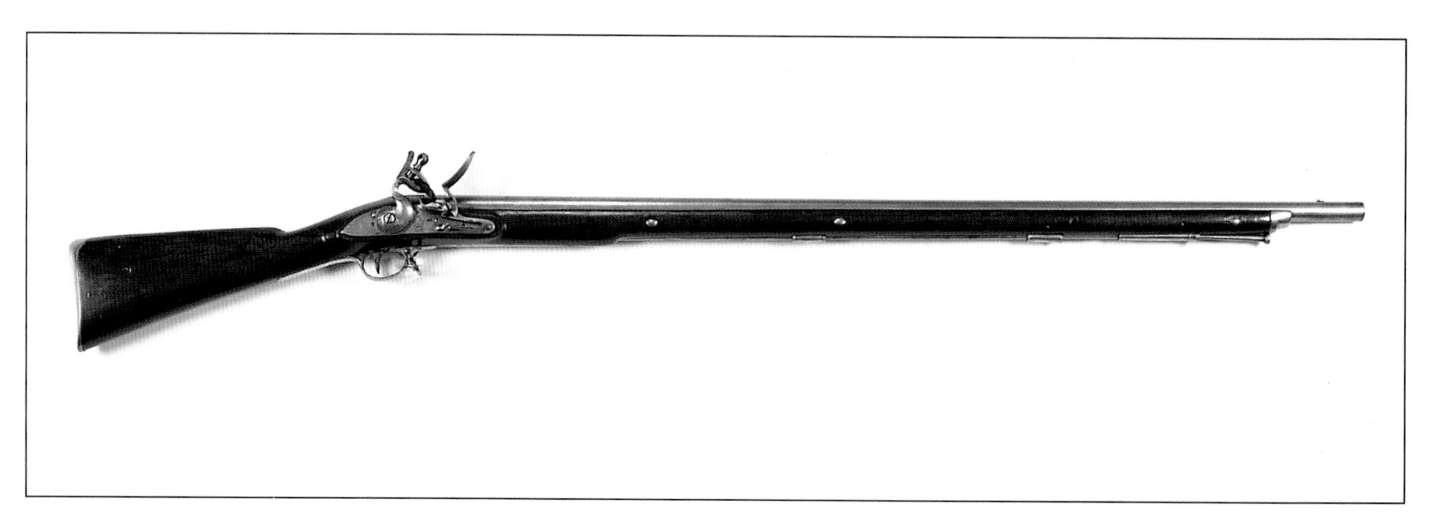

TYPE:	**10 BORE NEW LAND PATTERN BROWN BESS FLINTLOCK MUSKET**
MANUFACTURER:	Tower
DATE IN USE:	1803
COUNTRY OF MANUFACTURE:	UK
OPERATION:	muzzle loading, flintlock
LENGTH:	58 in/1,473 mm
WEIGHT:	10.5 lb/4.77 kg
EFFECTIVE RANGE:	109 yd/100 m

The New Land Pattern Musket was of better quality than the cheap India Pattern which was already in service. However, although issued from 1803, it did not entirely replace earlier models.

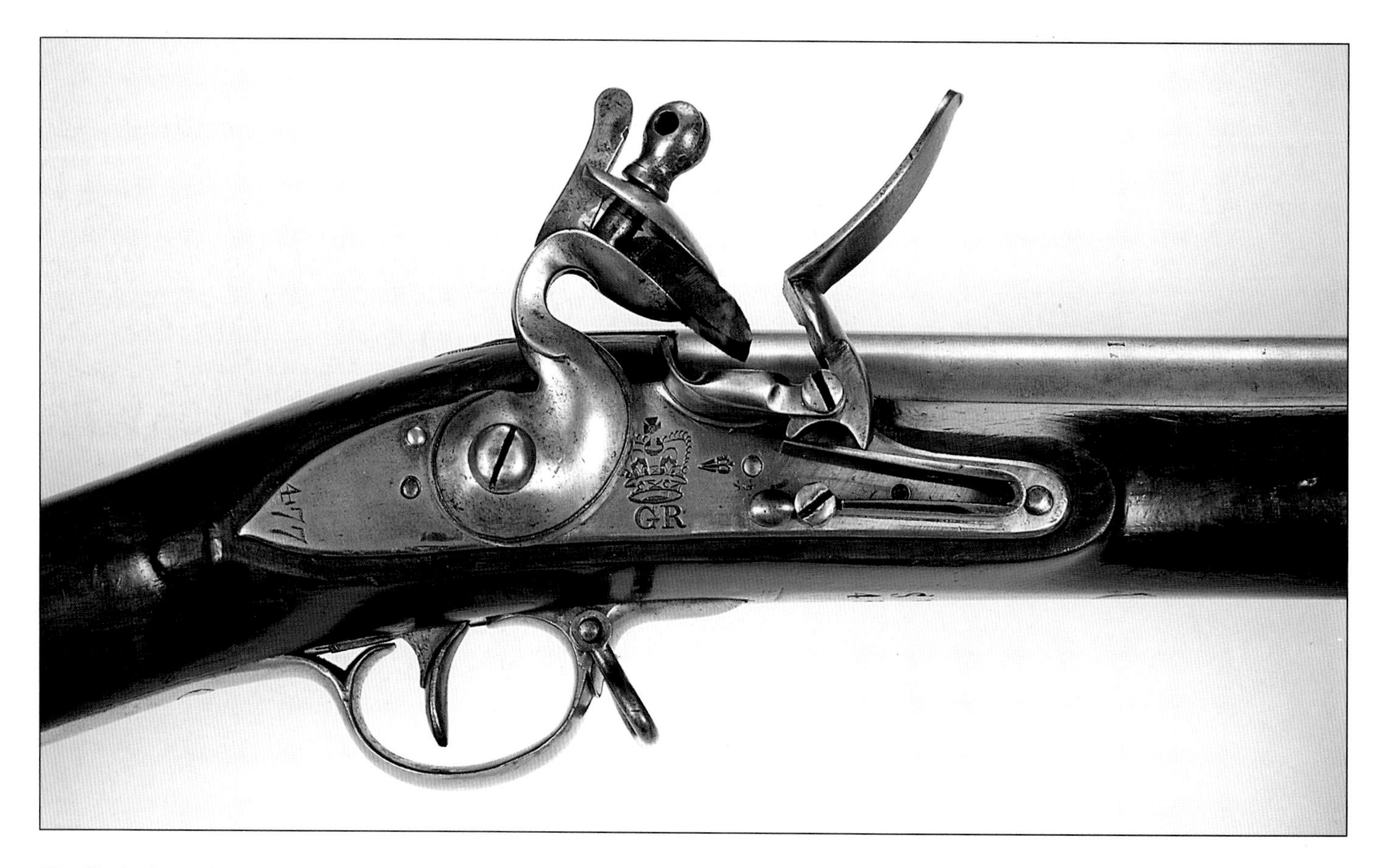

The flintlock was loaded first by tearing off the end of the cartridge and placing a quantity of black powder in the priming of the pan before being closed. The remaining powder would then be poured down the barrel. This was followed by the ball and then the cartridge paper. These would be pushed down the barrel by a ram rod to ensure that they were firmly pressed at the base of the barrel. The flint would then be cocked, the trigger squeezed and the flint would then strike the steel while simultaneously opening the priming pan. The resulting sparks would ignite the priming powder in the pan which in turn would ignite the main charge which forces the ball out.

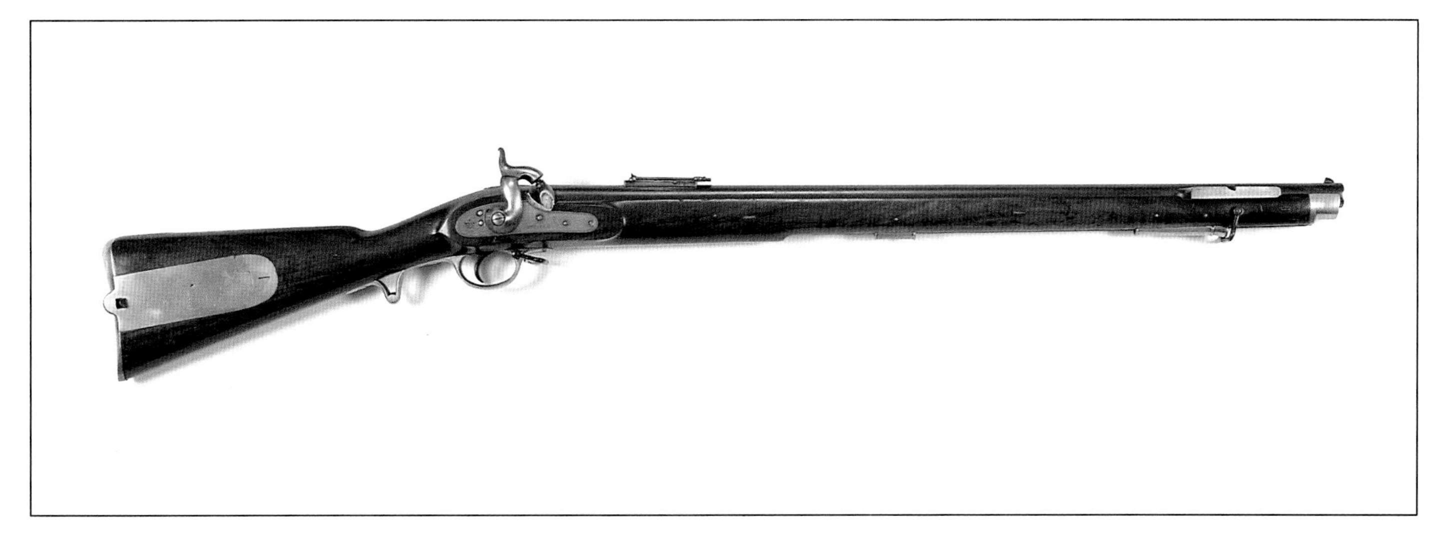

TYPE:	**.704 IN BRUNSWICK RIFLE**
MANUFACTURER:	Enfield
DATE IN USE:	1838
COUNTRY OF MANUFACTURE:	UK
OPERATION:	muzzle loading, percussion cap
LENGTH:	45.9 in/1,166 mm
WEIGHT:	9.75 lb/4.23 kg
EFFECTIVE RANGE:	251 yd/230 m (sights to 197 yd/180 m and 295 yd/270 m)

This percussion lock rifle replaced the Baker in British service from 1838. It was their first percussion cap rifle. The barrel was constructed with a double groove and fired a belted ball shot. This belted ball was inherently unstable and was particularly subject to cross winds. The Brunswick remained standard for the British rifle corps until 1851 and was then being replaced by the Minié. It served until 1870 with the Indian Army. This particular rifle has been fitted with an experimental back sight.

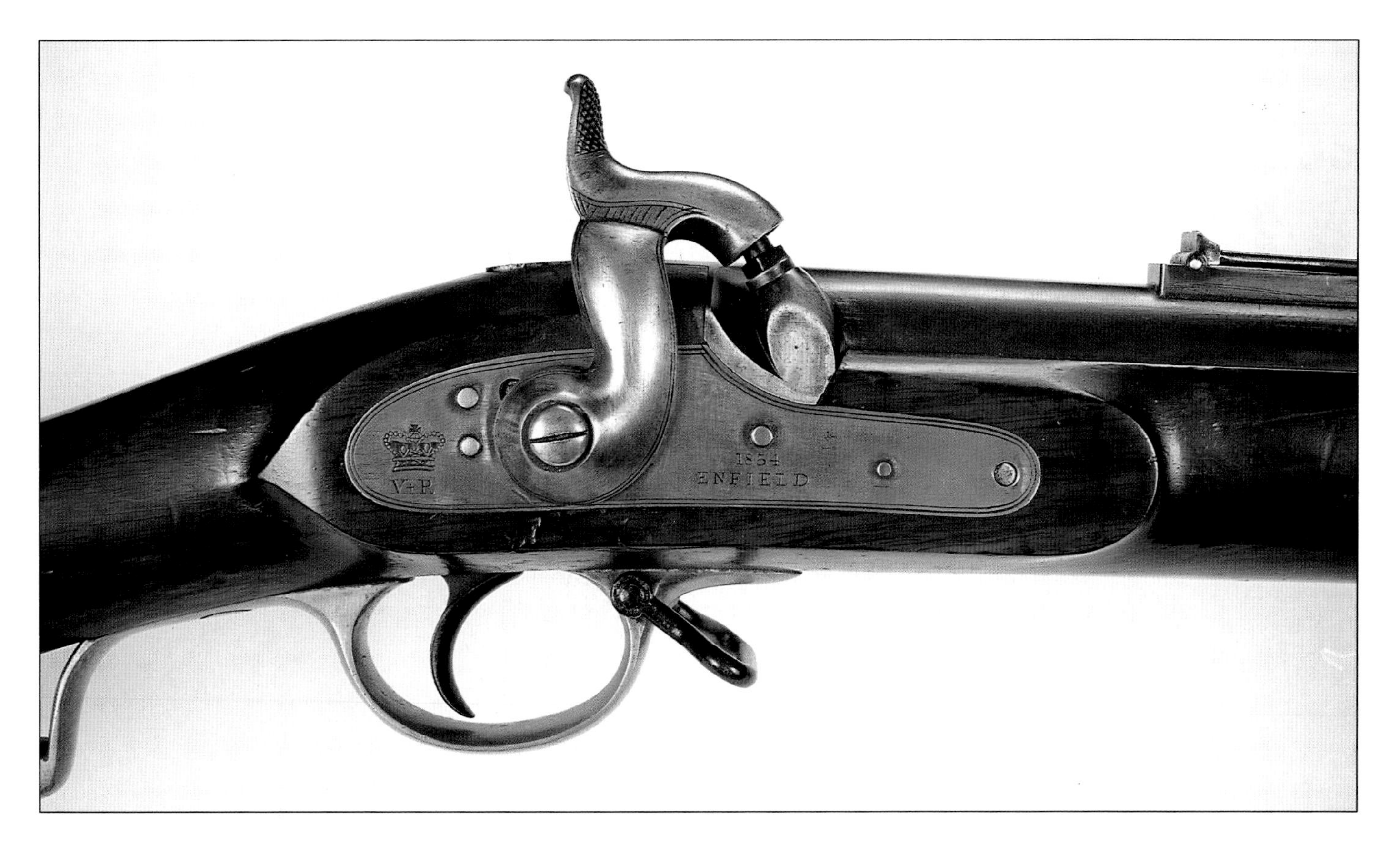

The percussion lock, in its final form, consisted of a small copper cap containing fulminate of mercury. This was placed on a nipple. When hit by the hammer, the fulminate exploded and the flame from the explosion travelled through the touch hole and ignited the main charge.

TYPE:	**.45 IN SIX-BARREL PEPPER-BOX**
MANUFACTURER:	Turner
DATE IN USE:	1840
COUNTRY OF MANUFACTURE:	UK
OPERATION:	muzzle loading, percussion cap
FEED:	6 rounds
LENGTH:	9.25 in/235 mm
WEIGHT:	2 lb/.91 kg
EFFECTIVE RANGE:	close quarters

This pepper-box pistol was constructed by Thomas Turner of Reading and was fired by means of the percussion cap. It was one of the first types of revolving pistol.

TYPE:	**.41 IN SIX-BARREL, SELF ACTING PEPPER-BOX PISTOL**
MANUFACTURER:	J R Cooper of London
DATE IN USE:	1840
COUNTRY OF MANUFACTURE:	UK
OPERATION:	muzzle loading, percussion cap
FEED:	6 round
LENGTH:	7.75 in/197 mm
WEIGHT:	1.5 lb/0.68 kg
EFFECTIVE RANGE:	close quarters

This cased pepper-box pistol was built by JR Cooper in 1840. He also designed and patented a firing system using percussion tubes which were inserted centrally into the bores and gave a strong and certain ignition. This six-barrel pepper-box is a good quality example of a percussion pistol.

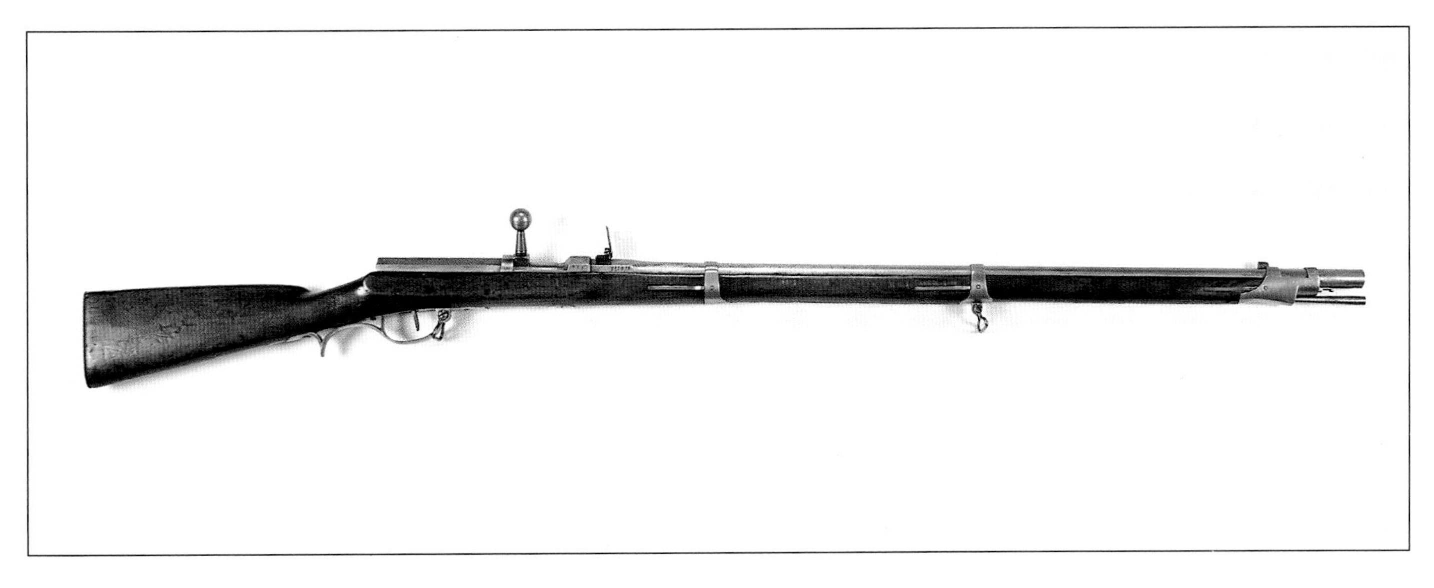

TYPE:	**15.43 MM ZUNDNADELGEWEHR (NEEDLE FIRE) M1841 RIFLE**
MANUFACTURER:	Spandau
DATE IN USE:	1848
COUNTRY OF MANUFACTURE:	Prussia
OPERATION:	bolt action, needle fire
LENGTH:	55.2 in/1,402 mm
WEIGHT:	10.5 lb/4.76 kg
EFFECTIVE RANGE:	328 yd/300 m (sights to 437 yd/400 m)

The Dreyse needle fire rifle was first issued to the Prussian Army in 1848. It demonstrated its devastating firepower against the Danes and Austrians.

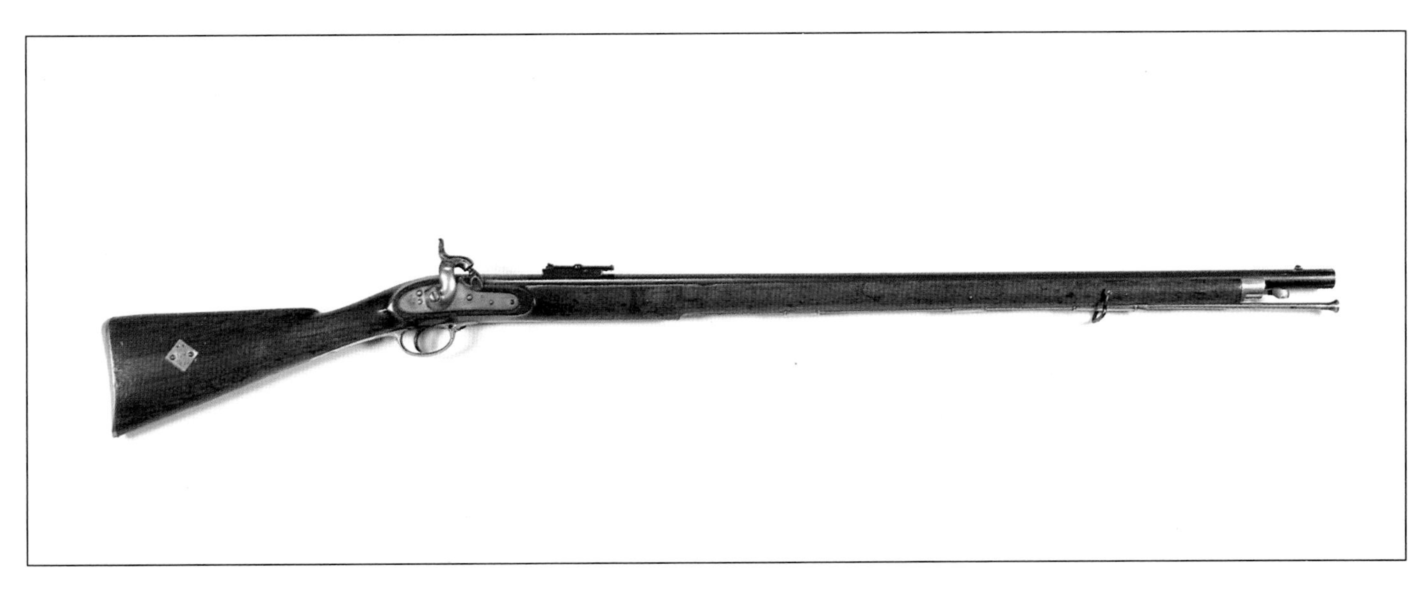

TYPE:	**.702 IN MINIÉ RIFLED MUSKET**
MANUFACTURER:	Tower
DATE IN USE:	1852
COUNTRY OF MANUFACTURE:	UK
OPERATION:	muzzle loading, percussion lock
LENGTH:	54.3 in/1,379 mm
WEIGHT:	9.25 lb/4.20 kg
EFFECTIVE RANGE:	871 yd/800 m (sights to 897 yd/820 m)

Two Frenchmen, Minié and Delvigne, designed the Minié system, the crux of which was a bullet that could be easily loaded like the old musket ball but, on firing, would expand to create an effective gas seal, at the same time seating on the rifling. This was achieved by using a bullet with a tapered chamber in the base and fitted in the base was a plug. When the charge was fired the force would push the plug into the base. Subsequent Minié Type bullets dispensed with the plug.

The Minié was also the first issue rifle for the British Infantry. By 1853 it was being replaced by the Enfield Pattern 1853. It was used in the Crimea where the ratio of Minié to Pattern 1853 was about three to one.

TYPE:	**.577 IN MODEL 1853 RIFLE**
MANUFACTURER:	Enfield
DATE IN USE:	1853
COUNTRY OF MANUFACTURE:	UK
OPERATION:	muzzle loading, percussion cap
LENGTH:	54.5 in/1,384 mm
WEIGHT:	8.75 lb/3.97 kg
EFFECTIVE RANGE:	984 yd/900 m (sights 500 yd/457 m to 800 yd/730 m)

This is a reduced calibre form of the Minié which it replaced. It had three groove rifling and could group to 4 inches at 100 yards. The adoption of the 1853 Pattern of Enfield rifles and carbines meant that at last the British Army was moving towards standardising on its weapon choice. The Model 1853 was used in the Crimean War, Indian Mutiny and American Civil War.

TYPE:	**54 BORE REVOLVER**
MANUFACTURER:	Deane-Adams
DATE IN USE:	1853
COUNTRY OF MANUFACTURE:	UK
OPERATION:	double-action (see also below)
LENGTH:	12.3 in/315 mm
WEIGHT:	2.2 lb/1 kg
EFFECTIVE RANGE:	close quarters

This revolver was originally constructed as a 54 bore, muzzle loaded percussion weapon in 1853. Around 1865 it was converted to take a .44 in centre fire cartridge. This involved replacing the cylinder and either modifying or replacing the hammer. The result was a vastly superior revolver.

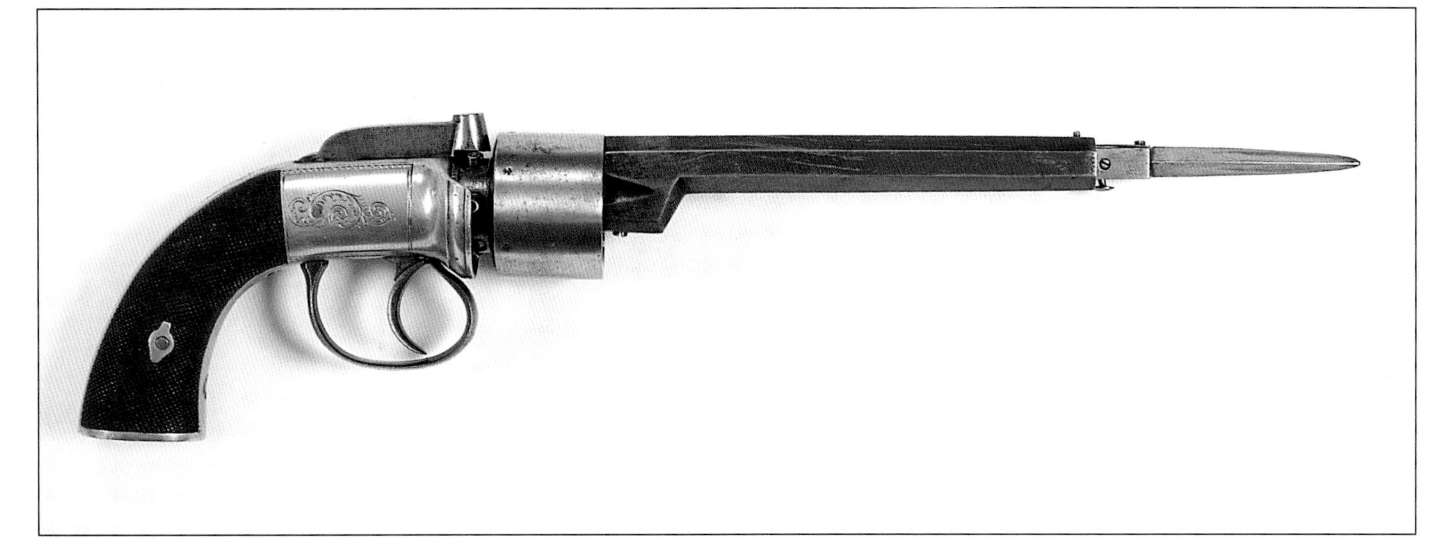

TYPE:	**.39 IN TRANSITIONAL IMPROVED REVOLVER**
MANUFACTURER:	not known
DATE IN USE:	1854
COUNTRY OF MANUFACTURE:	UK
OPERATION:	muzzle loading, percussion cap
FEED:	6 round cylinder
LENGTH:	12 in/305 mm (15.5 in/384 mm overall)
WEIGHT:	2.06 lb/0.94 kg
EFFECTIVE RANGE:	close quarters

The transitional weapons evolved during a period when traditional pepper-box manufacturers were attempting to supply a market which had been created by the Colt. The revolver was a compromise between the pepper-box and the Colt, and so did not infringe the Colt patent. This particular transitional revolver is fitted with a bayonet.

TYPE:	**.44 IN NO 2 DRAGOON REVOLVER**
MANUFACTURER:	Colt
DATE IN USE:	1855
COUNTRY OF MANUFACTURE:	USA
OPERATION:	single-action, pin fire
FEED:	6 round cylinder
LENGTH:	13.5 in/343 mm
WEIGHT:	3.88 lb/1.76 kg
EFFECTIVE RANGE:	close quarters

Colonel Samuel Colt's influence on the course of history of the handgun is unequalled by any other individual. He was also an excellent businessman in that he produced the right product at the right time and successfully marketed his product at an affordable price. Although he had a shaky start with his first revolver, the Paterson, his success commenced with the introduction of the Colt Walker Dragoon series. This No 2 Dragoon Revolver is also known as the Old Model Army Revolver.

TYPE:	.45 IN PERCUSSION REVOLVER
MANUFACTURER:	Deane-Adams
DATE IN USE:	1856
COUNTRY OF MANUFACTURE:	UK
OPERATION:	muzzle loading, percussion cap, single and double-action*
FEED:	5 rounds
LENGTH:	11.6 in/295 mm
WEIGHT:	2 lb/0.91 kg
EFFECTIVE RANGE:	close quarters

Following demonstrations by Colt at the Great Exhibition of 1851, the Navy and Army warmed slightly from their anti-revolver attitude. A trial was set up at the Woolwich Arsenal using the American Colt and British Adams revolvers. Although there was little difference between the two and the committee preferred the Adams, the War Office ordered the Colt with most being issued to the Navy.

Adams concentrated on improving his revolver to include the advantages of both his previous revolver and the Colt. The result was a revolver that could be used for either single or double-action* and was available in .45 and .50 calibre. Although the Colt was more accurate at longer distances the .50 had the capability of stopping anybody. The result was that the Army bought a quantity of the Deane-Adams revolver.

Events during the Crimean War and Sepoy Mutiny validated Adams' claims that the pistols were most effective during a charge by the enemy and that the Adams revolver had the edge over the Colt for speed of fire and stopping power.

*** Single action is where the hammer of the weapon must be cocked manually before applying pressure to the trigger to fire it.**
The double action weapon is usually operated by a straight pull on the trigger as well as by manually cocking the action.

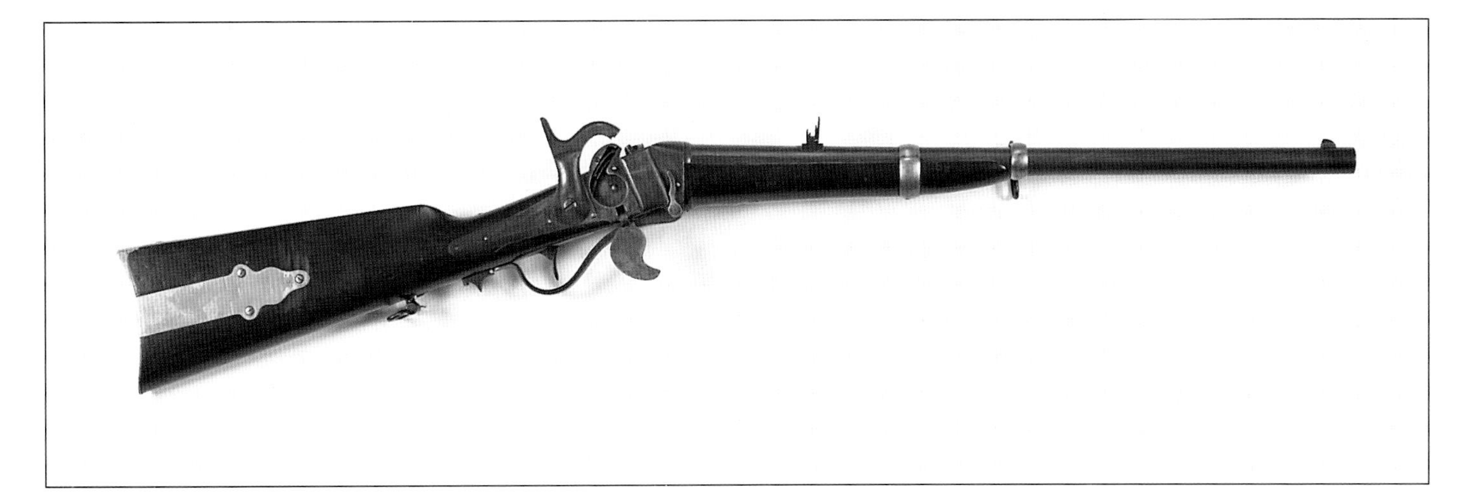

TYPE:	**.53 IN CAPPING BREECH LOADING CARBINE**
MANUFACTURER:	Sharps
DATE IN USE:	1857
COUNTRY OF MANUFACTURE:	USA
OPERATION:	breech-loading, tape primer
LENGTH:	37.1 in/942 mm
WEIGHT:	8 lb/3.63 kg
EFFECTIVE RANGE:	492 yd/450 m (sights 100 yd/91 m to 600 yd/548 m)

In 1857 the British Army began to experiment with breech-loading weapons. Various types were tested – the British Terry, the Westley Richards plus the American Sharps and the Greene amongst others. While the British selected the Westley Richards carbine for the cavalry, the Americans used the Terry and Sharps extensively during the American Civil War.

This Sharps breech-loading carbine makes use of the Maynard tape primer which was one of a variety of capping systems used by Sharps. Selected British cavalry units were issued with this type of rising breech block carbine for troop trials. The term 'Sharpshooter' originated from the infantry version of this carbine.

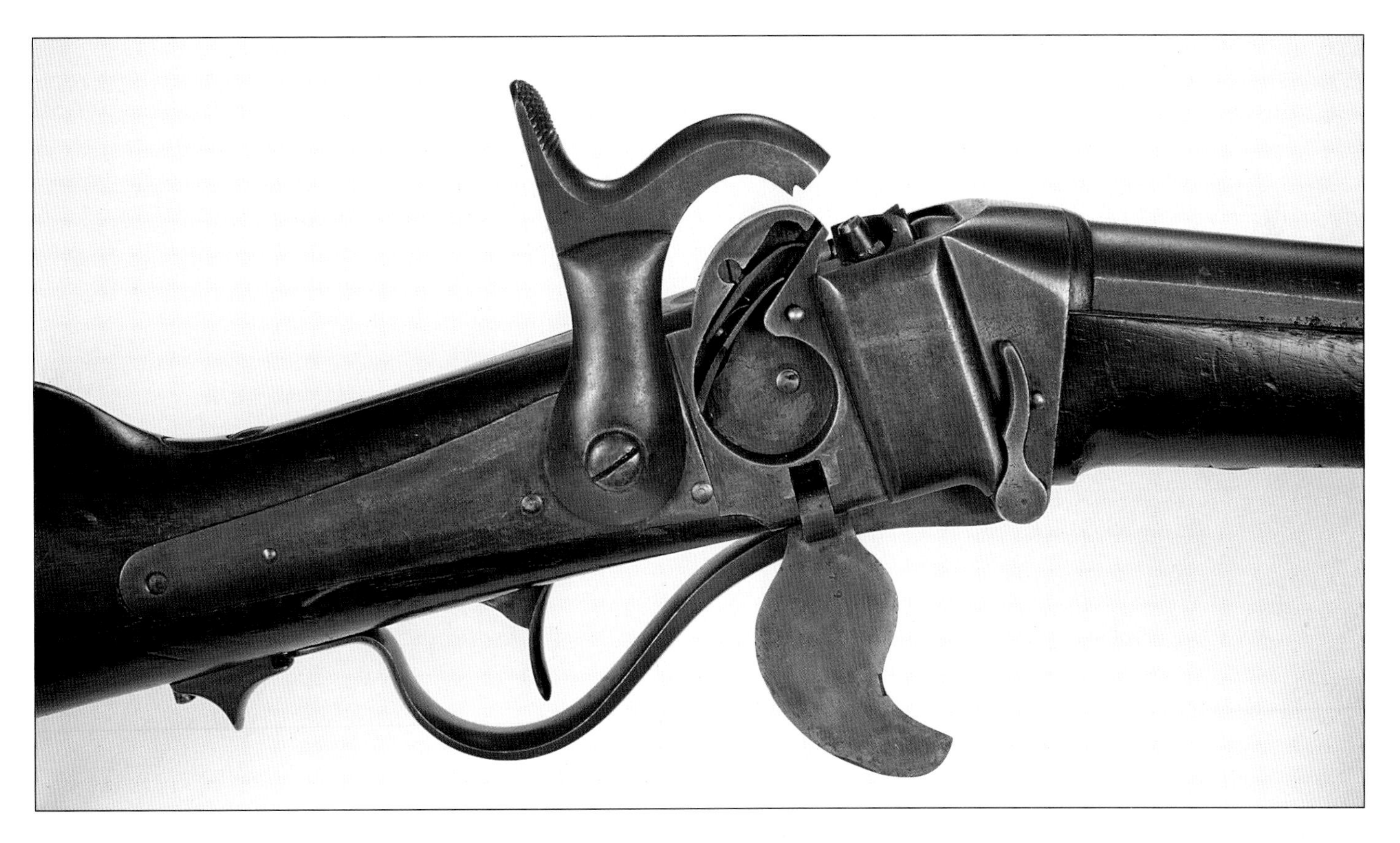

An alternative to the percussion cap was the paper cap. This comprised two layers of paper with the explosive sandwiched between. This resembled the modern toy cap pistols and utilised the flash to ignite the main charge.

TYPE:	**10.7 MM MODEL 1858 REVOLVER**
MANUFACTURER:	Lefaucheux
DATE IN USE:	1858
COUNTRY OF MANUFACTURE:	France
OPERATION:	single-action, pin fire
FEED:	6 round cylinder
LENGTH:	11.5 in/292 mm
WEIGHT:	2.38 lb/1.08 kg
EFFECTIVE RANGE:	close quarters

Lefaucheux was credited with inventing the first practical self primed metallic cartridge – the pin fired cartridge – in 1835. This consisted of a copper case which contained the igniter, main charge and a bullet. Initially these were joined by a paper tube but subsequently the metal case was extended up to the bullet. A hole was made in the wall of the case near to the base and a cardboard piece containing the percussion cap was inserted into the base of the case and a pin located through the hole. When loaded into the weapon, the action of the hammer hitting the pin would ignite the percussion cap and thus fire the charge. The Model 1858 was adopted by the French Navy and became the first pin fire hand-gun to be adopted officially for service by any military power.

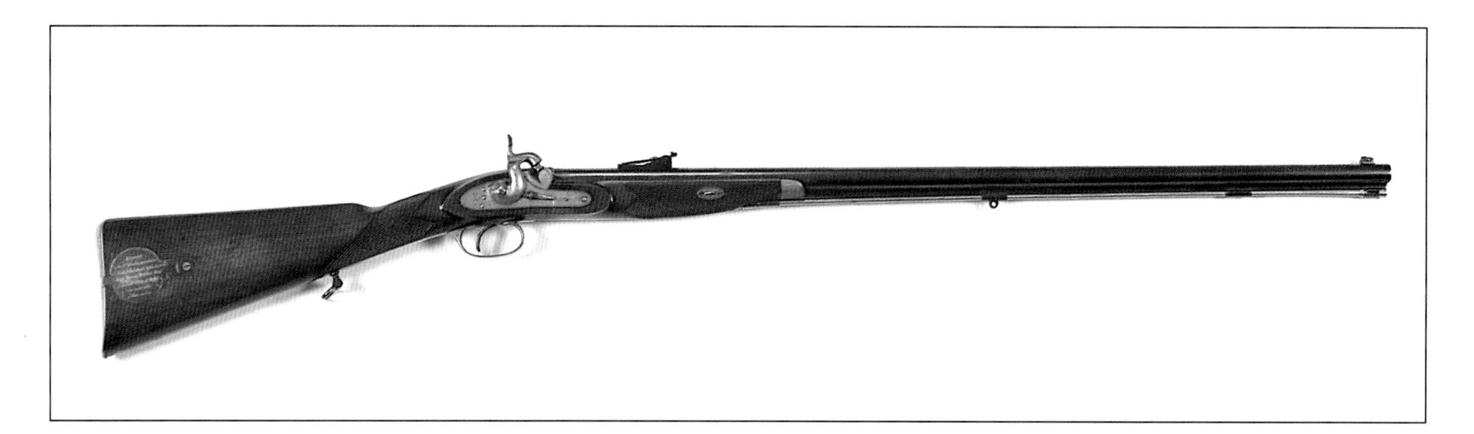

TYPE:	**.45 TARGET RIFLE**
MANUFACTURER:	Whitworth
DATE IN USE:	1859
COUNTRY OF MANUFACTURE:	UK
OPERATION:	muzzle loading, percussion cap
LENGTH:	48.6 in/1,234 mm
WEIGHT:	8 lb/3.63 kg
EFFECTIVE RANGE:	984 yd/900 m (sight 500 yd/457 m to 900 yd/822 m)

In 1857 a rifle designed by Sir Joseph Whitworth was tested at Hythe. It was able to out-gun the Enfield with a high degree of accuracy beyond 900 m. It owed its accuracy to its hexagonal bore and the very accurately moulded bullets. It was used by the Rifle Brigade for a while but was not adopted due to its tendency to foul the bore. Many were purchased by the Confederate States of America and performed well in the hands of marksmen during the American Civil War.

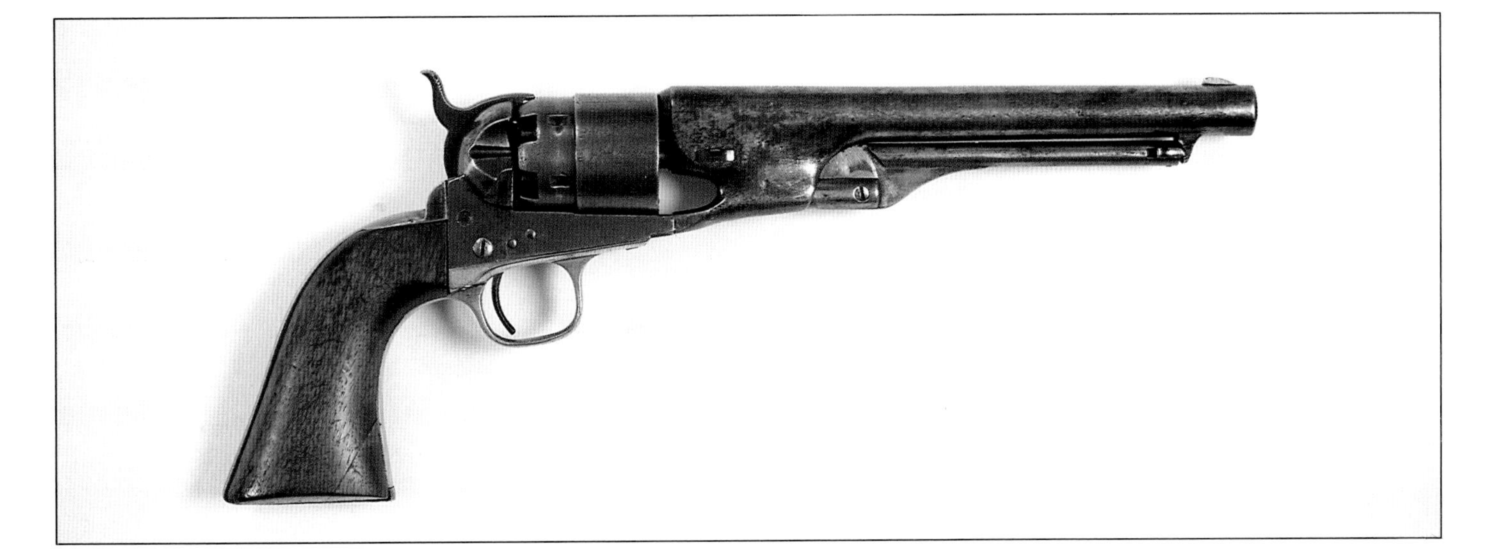

TYPE:	**.44 IN NEW MODEL ARMY REVOLVER**
MANUFACTURER:	Colt
DATE IN USE:	1860
COUNTRY OF MANUFACTURE:	USA
OPERATION:	muzzle loaded, single-action
FEED:	6 rounds
LENGTH:	13.25 in/337 mm
WEIGHT:	2.69 lb/1.22 kg
EFFECTIVE RANGE:	close quarters

In 1860 Colt introduced the New Model Army Revolver. This was also known as the New Model Holster Revolver. It utilised the same frame as the Model 1851 Naval revolver but with the front part cut away to take a rebated cylinder to accommodate the .44 calibre bullet. This is the cap and ball revolver which set the pattern for revolvers to the present day.

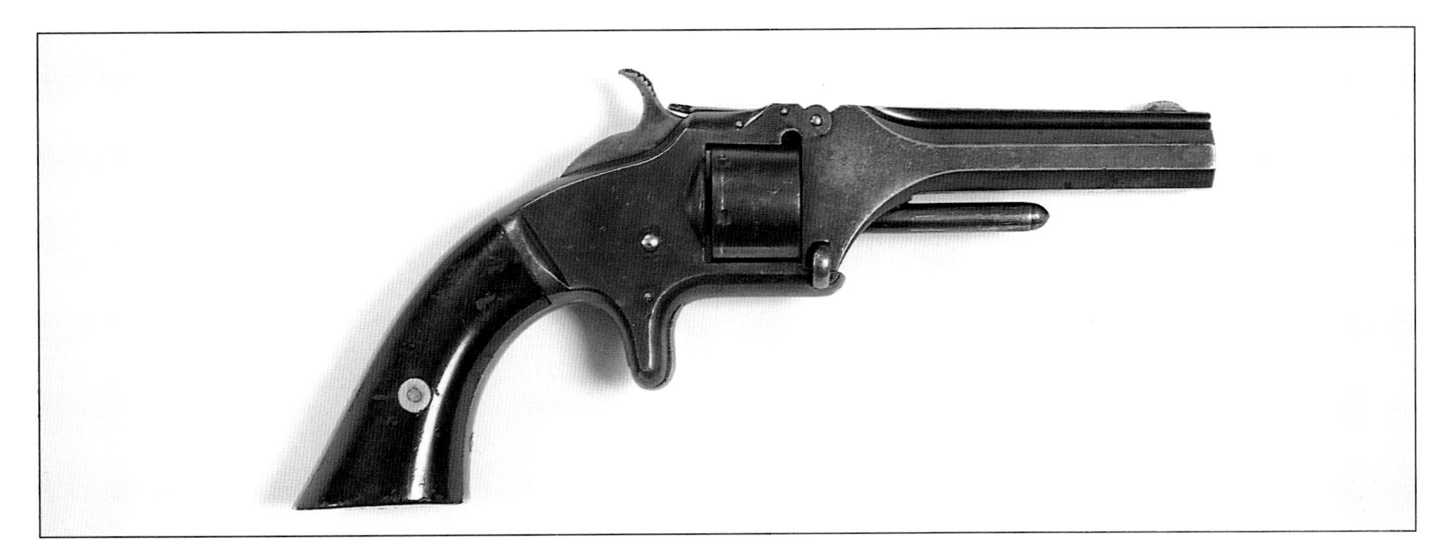

TYPE:	**.22 IN MODEL NO.1**
MANUFACTURER:	Smith & Wesson
DATE IN USE:	1860
COUNTRY OF MANUFACTURE:	USA
OPERATION:	single-action, rimfire
FEED:	7 round cylinder
LENGTH:	7.25 in/184.14 mm
WEIGHT:	0.75 lb/0.34 kg
EFFECTIVE RANGE:	close quarters

Smith and Wesson bought up a patent for a bored through cylinder. This made way for the loading of a complete cartridge through the rear end of the cylinder for the first time. The Model No.1 used a short .22 in rimfire round which had a copper case. These had a tendency to bulge on firing and so a recoil plate was designed which supported the cartridge heads, thus preventing the jamming. Once fired, the barrel hinges upward and the cylinder can be removed. The spent cartridges are lifted out. Those stuck in can be pushed out using a rod which protrudes from under the front of the barrel lug.

TYPE:	**.41 IN DERRINGER DOUBLE-BARRELLED PISTOL**
MANUFACTURER:	Remington Small Arms Co
DATE IN USE:	1861
COUNTRY OF MANUFACTURE:	USA
OPERATION:	single-action, percussion cap
FEED:	2 round
LENGTH:	4.9 in/124 mm
WEIGHT:	0.8 lb/0.36 kg
EFFECTIVE RANGE:	close quarters

By 1825 Derringer was utilising the percussion cap in his pistols and this resulted in a demand for the pistol, as it was now small enough to be carried in the pocket without attracting attention. The Derringer was a highly popular single and double shot pistol.

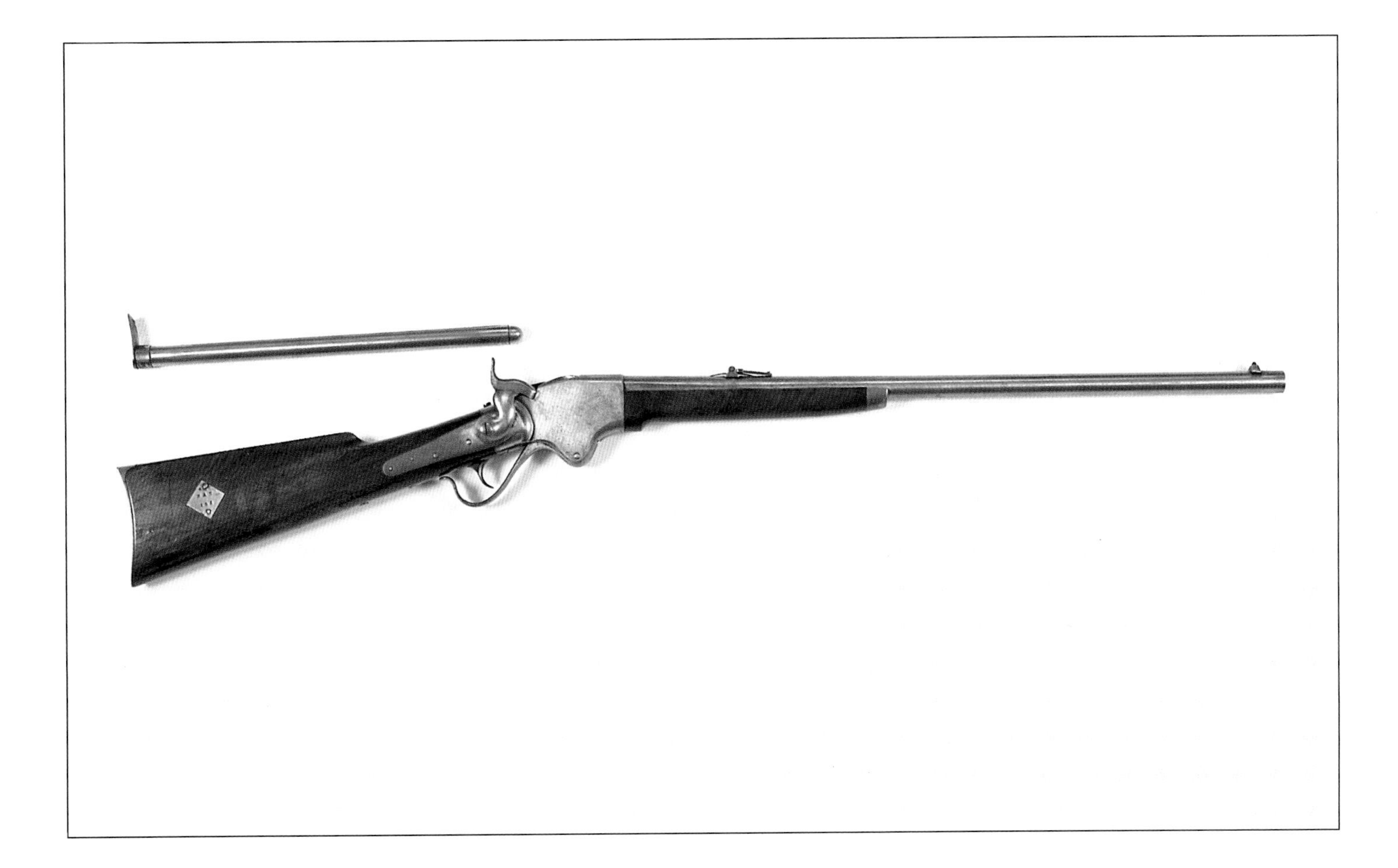

TYPE:	**.44 IN SPENCER REPEATING CARBINE**
MANUFACTURER:	Spencer Repeating Rifle Co
DATE IN USE:	1862
COUNTRY OF MANUFACTURE:	USA
OPERATION:	lever action, rolling block
FEED:	7 round tube magazine in butt
LENGTH:	42.5 in/1,079 mm
WEIGHT:	9 lb/4.08 kg
EFFECTIVE RANGE:	300 yd/275 m

The Spencer was the first successful repeating rifle. Designed before the beginning of the American Civil War, when rifle producers were concentrating on muzzle loading percussion rifles, Spencer had difficulty in getting the authorities to take his idea seriously. Following intervention by President Lincoln, trials in 1861 led to substantial orders, to the extent that demand soon exceeded the manufacturing capacity. Later Civil War issues were in .52 or .50 calibres.

The Spencer was a breech-loading rifle using rimfire metallic cartridges. Its revolutionary concept was the fact that it could store seven of these cartridges in a tube within the stock and by operating a lever could load these cartridges in quick succession. This was achieved by depressing a lever that doubled as the trigger guard. This falling breech-block motion ejected the empty case and the raising of the lever gave a rotating motion which fed the next round into the chamber. Once cocked, the trigger was squeezed and the cycle repeated until the ammunition needed replenishment.

When the war finished Spencer's financial backers withdrew support, surplus stock was purchased by Oliver Winchester and ensured the demise of his competition. In 1877, when his Winchester 1866 was used very effectively against the Russians at Plevna, the Winchester was the only repeating rifle available to fulfil new requirements.

TYPE:	.45 IN WESTLEY-RICHARDS 'MONKEY TAIL' CARBINE
MANUFACTURER:	Enfield
DATE IN USE:	1863
COUNTRY OF MANUFACTURE:	UK
OPERATION:	breech-loading, single capping
LENGTH:	35.25 in/895 mm
WEIGHT:	6 lb/2.72 kg
EFFECTIVE RANGE:	383 yd/350 m

The Westley-Richards 'monkey tail' carbine was fitted with a trap behind the barrel which was lifted to load the cartridge. This was the principal British cavalry carbine issued until 1871 when it was replaced by the carbine version of the Martini.

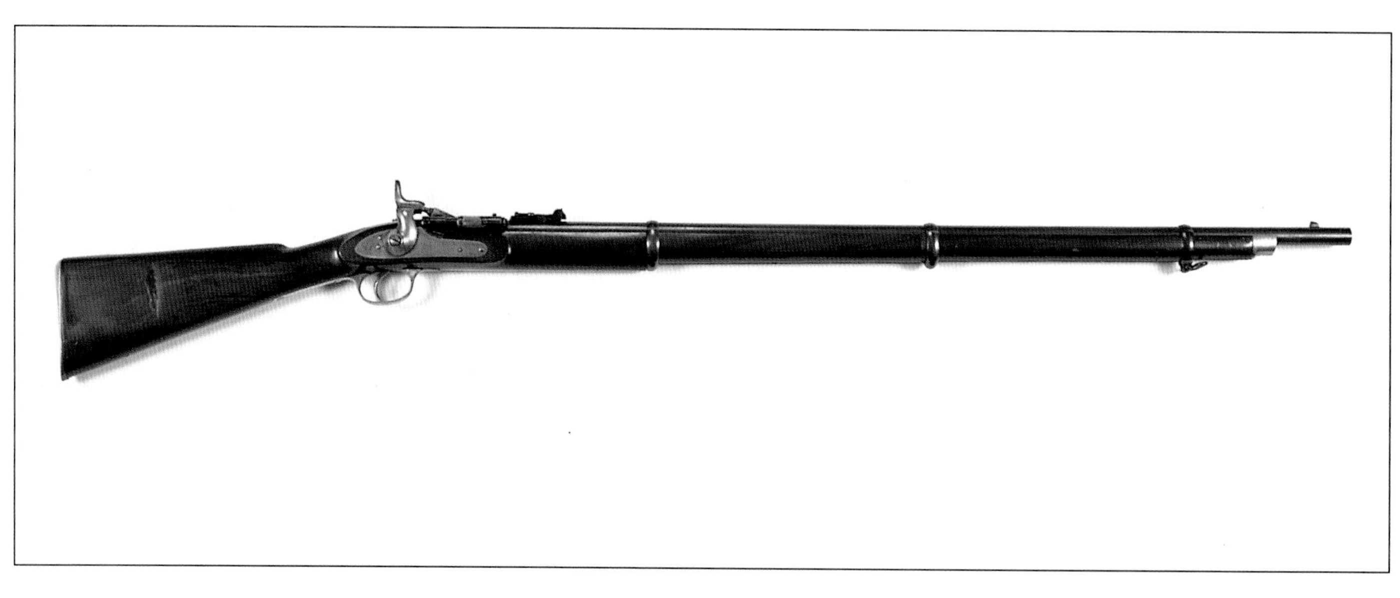

TYPE:	.577 SNIDER/ENFIELD CONVERSION
MANUFACTURER:	Enfield
DATE IN USE:	1865
COUNTRY OF MANUFACTURE:	USA (UK)
OPERATION:	breech-loading, centre fire cartridge
LENGTH:	53.5 in/1,359 mm
WEIGHT:	8.5 lb/3.8 kg
EFFECTIVE RANGE:	492 yd/450 m (sights 500 yd/457 m to 800 yd/731 m)

In common with most countries, Britain had large stocks of muzzle loading rifles. A variety of conversions to breech-loading were adopted in Europe and America. Britain chose the American Snider as a stop-gap for her Infantry before the introduction of the Martini-Henry from 1871. However, it remained in service as late as 1900.

TYPE:	**.44 IN MODEL 1866 CARBINE**
MANUFACTURER:	Winchester
DATE IN USE:	1866
COUNTRY OF MANUFACTURE:	USA
OPERATION:	lever action, repeater
FEED:	13 round magazine
LENGTH:	38.8 in/986 mm
WEIGHT:	7.3 lb/3.31 kg
EFFECTIVE RANGE:	300 yd/275 m

The .44 in Winchester was based on Henry's Patent Rifle but with improvements by Nelson King. The most important of these was the loading gate which enabled the magazine to be loaded from the rear end.

In 1877, a Russian army massed before the Turkish defences at Plevna. As they advanced, the Turks fired their longer range, single shot Peabody-Martinis to the detriment of the Russians. As they progressed to within a few hundred yards the Turks changed their rifles and as the Russians attempted their final charge they were cut down by the firepower provided by 30,000 Turkish .44 Winchesters. A few weeks later a similar attack was mounted with the same results. All told, some 30,000 Russian men were lost. This result sparked off a new requirement for repeating rifles all around Europe.

TYPE:	**11 MM MODEL 1866 CHASSEPOT RIFLE**
MANUFACTURER:	Imperiale
DATE IN USE:	1867
COUNTRY OF MANUFACTURE:	France
OPERATION:	bolt action, needle fire
LENGTH:	50.75 in/1,288 mm
WEIGHT:	8.69 lb/3.94 kg
EFFECTIVE RANGE:	437 yd/400 m (sights to 437 yd/400 m and 1312 yd/1200 m)

The Chassepot bolt action, breech-loading rifle was adopted by the French Army in 1866 and remained the standard until 1874. It had an improved version of needle fire action compared to the Dreyse. It located the primer at the base of the cartridge rather than against the bullet, which therefore required a shorter firing pin. Also introduced was a rubber disk which, although requiring frequent changes, provided a more efficient gas seal.

TYPE:	**10.4 MM VETTERLI VITALI MAGAZINE RIFLE**
MANUFACTURER:	Brescia (Vetterli)
DATE IN USE:	1867
COUNTRY OF MANUFACTURE:	Italy (Switzerland)
OPERATION:	bolt action, breech-loading
FEED:	4 round magazine
LENGTH:	52.1 in/1,323 mm
WEIGHT:	8.5 lb/3.86 kg
EFFECTIVE RANGE:	1,094 yd/1,000 m (sights to 1,094 yd/1,000 m)

Although Switzerland is a neutral country, it has always required an effective defence. As a result the Swiss have a continual appraisal of their own and other nations' military developments. The introduction of the breech-loading Dreyse Needle-Gun by the Prussians was instrumental in the defeat of the Danes and Austrians in the 1860s and the Swiss were determined to adopt a rifle that could enable them to out-shoot this powerful weapon.

Frederick Vetterli successfully designed a bolt action repeating rifle using a copper metallic cartridge. It took a little time before the effectiveness of this system was appreciated, but in 1867 initial production of the Vetterli commenced following its adoption by the Swiss Confederation and subsequently by the Italian Army.

This particular rifle was built in Italy by Brescia in 1878 and converted with the Vetterli Vitali magazine mechanism in 1887. It was part of Carson's UVF armoury of 1912.

TYPE:	**.38 IN AND .476 IN FOUR-BARRELLED PISTOLS**
MANUFACTURER:	Lancaster
DATE IN USE:	1882
COUNTRY OF MANUFACTURE:	UK
OPERATION:	brake action, revolving striker
FEED:	4 rounds in separate barrels
LENGTH:	11 in/279 mm (.476 in pistol)
WEIGHT:	2.56 lb/1.16 kg
EFFECTIVE RANGE:	close quarters

The two and four barrel Lancaster pistols were designed to overcome the unreliability of the conventional revolver which often fouled from using black powder cartridges and dirty operating conditions. The only moving part of the Lancaster was the centre firing striker.

The striker is attached to the front end of the grooved cylinder. Pressure on the trigger draws the cylinder back and also causes it to rotate through 90 degrees, thus bringing the striker into line with each chamber in succession.

Charles Lancaster was a believer in the oval bore method of rifling. These pistols have been constructed with a twisted oval bore as were many of his pistols.

TYPE:	**.450 IN MARTINI-HENRY RIFLE**
MANUFACTURER:	Enfield
DATE IN USE:	1887
COUNTRY OF MANUFACTURE:	UK
OPERATION:	breech-loading, pivoted block
LENGTH:	48.8 in/1,239 mm
WEIGHT:	8.57 lb/3.97 kg
EFFECTIVE RANGE:	383 yd/350 m (sights 500 yd/457 m to 1,400 yd/1,280 m)

The Martini-Henry was adopted in 1871 to replace the large number of stop-gap Snider converted Enfields. The original rifle was re-barrelled in parallel with change to the .303 ammunition. As a consequence the Martini actions occur with a wide variety of calibres and rifling. Although subsequently replaced by the Lee bolt action in the British Infantry, the Martini actions remained in service well into the 1900s.

This Martini-Henry is fitted with a long lever to aid extraction.

The selection of the Martini Henry as the new British service rifle brought together Martini's action and Henry's rifling and utilised the rolled/coiled brass cartridges.

TYPE:	**.303 LEE METFORD RIFLE MK.I**
MANUFACTURER:	not known
DATE IN USE:	1888
COUNTRY OF MANUFACTURE:	UK
OPERATION:	bolt action
FEED:	8 round magazine
LENGTH:	48.74 in/1,238 mm
WEIGHT:	9 lb/4.09 kg
EFFECTIVE RANGE:	984 yd/900 m (sights 500 yd/457 m to 1,600 yd/1,462 m)

In 1888 the British decided to adopt the .303 calibre bolt action magazine rifle. It incorporated Lee's bolt mechanism with Metford's rifling. The introduction of cordite as a propellant soon made it clear that the Metford rifling was too shallow, so in 1895 the existing rifle was re-barrelled and issued as the Lee Enfield.

TYPE:	**.455 IN NO.1 MK.II REVOLVER**
MANUFACTURER:	Webley & Scott
DATE IN USE:	1894
COUNTRY OF MANUFACTURE:	UK
OPERATION:	single and double-action
FEED:	6 round cylinder
LENGTH:	9.25 in/235 mm
WEIGHT:	2.25 lb/1.02 kg
EFFECTIVE RANGE:	close quarters

The Webley & Scott Mk.I originally entered service with the British in 1887. Over the years various Marks and variations have evolved. However, in 1926 they were redesignated the No.1 revolver and retained the original Mark No. Due to a shortage of pistols in World War Two the British re-issued some of the earlier models. The British Army used .455 Webley revolvers for some 60 years. This revolver, which fired the centre fire cartridge, has changed little since its introduction more than 100 years ago.

TYPE:	**7.92 MM GEWEHR M1898 'MAUSER'**
MANUFACTURER:	Spandau
DATE IN USE:	1898
COUNTRY OF MANUFACTURE:	Germany
OPERATION:	bolt action
FEED:	5 round magazine
LENGTH:	48.5 in/1,232 mm
WEIGHT:	8.5 lb/3.86 kg
EFFECTIVE RANGE:	984 yd/900 m (sights to 2,187 yd/2,000 m)

The Model 98 Rifle was introduced in 1898 and was one of the most successful bolt action rifles produced. This resulted in the action being used subsequently by most countries of the world.

The Model 98 rifle was the principal rifle for the German Army in World War One and in a shorter version in World War Two. It was built in a number of variations including the carbine.

FROM MANUAL TO SELF-LOADING

1901-1944

The beginning of the 20th century saw a pattern of small-bore, bolt action magazine rifles becoming the primary weapon for the infantry soldier. Following trials the Short Magazine Lee-Enfield Mark I was adopted by the British Army in 1902 while the 1903 Springfield was adopted by the US the following year. While these high-velocity rifles might be sighted to 2,000 yd (1,829 m) they were largely ineffective at that distance and would normally be used at 500–600 yd (457–549 m) where their flat trajectory would ensure that the bullet did not need to rise above head height. Thus accurate sighting became unnecessary at these ranges.

The British experience of the Boer War increased their belief in firepower. With a treasury reluctant to purchase machine guns, it was decided to provide each soldier with thorough training in the theory and practical art of firing a rifle accurately.

When World War One broke out this training proved invaluable. The Germans launched mass attacks and it was only the accurate fire which the soldier could maintain at a rapid rate due to this training that ensured the lines were held. The rapid rate of fire even led some Germans to believe that the British were using massed machine guns. While the British were using the SMLE the Germans were equipped with the 1898 Mauser. The Germans also had large numbers of the Maxim machine gun while the British had smaller numbers of the Vickers machine gun.

It wasn't long before the war became static with the British superior rifle firepower matched by the German superior strength in machine guns. Massed attacks were attempted to break the stalemate only to be cut down by the machine guns. The problem for the British was that so many of the highly trained regulars were being shot and the need for urgent replacements had meant that they had not been given the same quality training. The brute force of the machine guns was overshadowing the skill of the rifle.

Specialist snipers made good use of the long range of the high-velocity rifle. When fitted with a telescopic sight and in the hands of a skilled marksman, during the period of trench warfare the enemy could be picked off whenever they were seen.

When the British Army first deployed the tank, the Germans had no means of defeating what was in effect a mobile machine gun post. The Germans, in a panic to produce a defence against this new weapon which was causing them some problems, designed an anti-tank rifle. This was little more than a scaled-up single shot rifle that fired a 13 mm hardened bullet, and it had limited success.

While the revolver had been the dominant hand weapon during the 1800s, the self-loading pistol was starting to see further development in Europe. By the beginning of World War One the British officers and some others including machine gunners were equipped with the Webley-Scott revolvers, although these were of little use except for close-quarters fighting such as trench raids. Many other countries had opted for the self-loading pistols.

Meanwhile, in America, the home of the revolver, Colt was producing a series of different automatic pistols. When the United States joined the Allies in World War One the 1911 Colt was used extensively, but when insufficient numbers of the Colt pistol were available the Smith & Wesson or Colt revolvers were issued in substantial numbers.

A successful development by the Germans but outside the scope of this book, was from the Luger/Mauser pistol. When fitted with a detachable stock, these self-loading pistols were found to be extremely useful for trench fighting. From this was developed the idea for the early sub-machine guns such as the Bergmann MP.18 which were capable of firing bursts and used the 32 round 'snail' magazine from the Luger. The sub-machine gun is a light machine gun that fires pistol ammunition. These entered service too late to have any real impact on World War One but were later successfully developed in many forms.

After World War One, the development of new weapons ceased with only a few exceptions. The old style training returned in an attempt to regain the previous high standards. Later developments in the UK only resulted in a simpler version of the Lee-Enfield – the Mark 4. Similarly, the Germans were introducing the KAR.98 which was a shortened version of their previous 1898 model. However, the Germans probably made the greatest development with the introduction of the MG.34 general purpose machine gun.

The Germans were also developing new pistols in the form of the Walther PP and PPK. Originally designed as police pistols, the PPK had a shorter barrel so that it could be concealed in the pocket of a plain clothes policeman. As World War Two approached these two pistols were issued to the military forces. These were followed by the P38 in the larger 9 mm calibre which was adopted as the basic German sidearm.

The Russian Tokarev introduced their automatic pistol which looked very similar to the .32 Colt and Browning, although the finish is not to the same standard due to the simplified production techniques.

In Belgium, the FN factory launched the 1935 Browning pistol which was a modification of a previous model but was to become one of the most widely used pistols in the world.

The Americans had designed a new self-loading rifle to be known as the Springfield M1 Garand. In 1936 this became the first self-loading rifle to be adopted by any army as their standard weapon. It was heavy but strong and reliable and as a result over 4,000,000 were built.

TYPE:	**.303 IN THORNYCROFT EXPERIMENTAL CARBINE**
MANUFACTURER:	Lee Enfield
DATE IN USE:	1901
COUNTRY OF MANUFACTURE:	UK
OPERATION:	bolt action
FEED:	5 round magazine
LENGTH:	38.9 in/988 mm
WEIGHT:	7 lb/3.18 kg
EFFECTIVE RANGE:	984 yd/900 m (sight to 2,000 yd/1,828 m)

The Boer War saw the introduction of mounted infantry who were armed with firearms and fought dismounted with rifles. The cavalry preferred the lance and sabre for 'shock actions' but Lord Robertson prevailed upon them to use firearms.

Thornycroft designed his magazine weapon with both cavalry and mounted infantry in mind, and it had the compact length desirable for a horseman. This new rifle achieved the characteristics of the shorter carbine but maintained the accuracy of a standard rifle by designing the mechanism such that the trigger is forward of the breech enabling a longer barrel for the same overall weapon length. This concept became known as the bullpup.

TYPE:	**.303 IN SHORT MAGAZINE LEE ENFIELD NO.1 MK.III* (SMLE)**
MANUFACTURER:	Enfield (BSA)
DATE IN USE:	1903
COUNTRY OF MANUFACTURE:	UK
OPERATION:	bolt action
FEED:	10 round magazine
LENGTH:	44 in/1,118 mm
WEIGHT:	8.62 lb/3.91 kg
EFFECTIVE RANGE:	492 yd/450m (sights 200 yd183 m to 1,500 yd/1,371 m)

The Short Magazine Lee Enfield (SMLE) was adopted after the South African War of 1899–1902 as a standard rifle. It was shorter than the original model Lee Enfield and was charger loaded.

Production of the No.1 rifle was introduced in 1903 and phased out when the No.4 rifle became available in World War Two. The Mk.III came into service in 1907 and was extensively used during World War One with some 3,000,000 being made. While large numbers of the No.1 rifles from World War One were repaired and upgraded to Mk.III, the SMLE Mk.III & Mk.III* continued in production by BSA until November 1943.

Overseas production continued in Australia and nearly 700,000 were also made in India where production finally terminated in 1955.

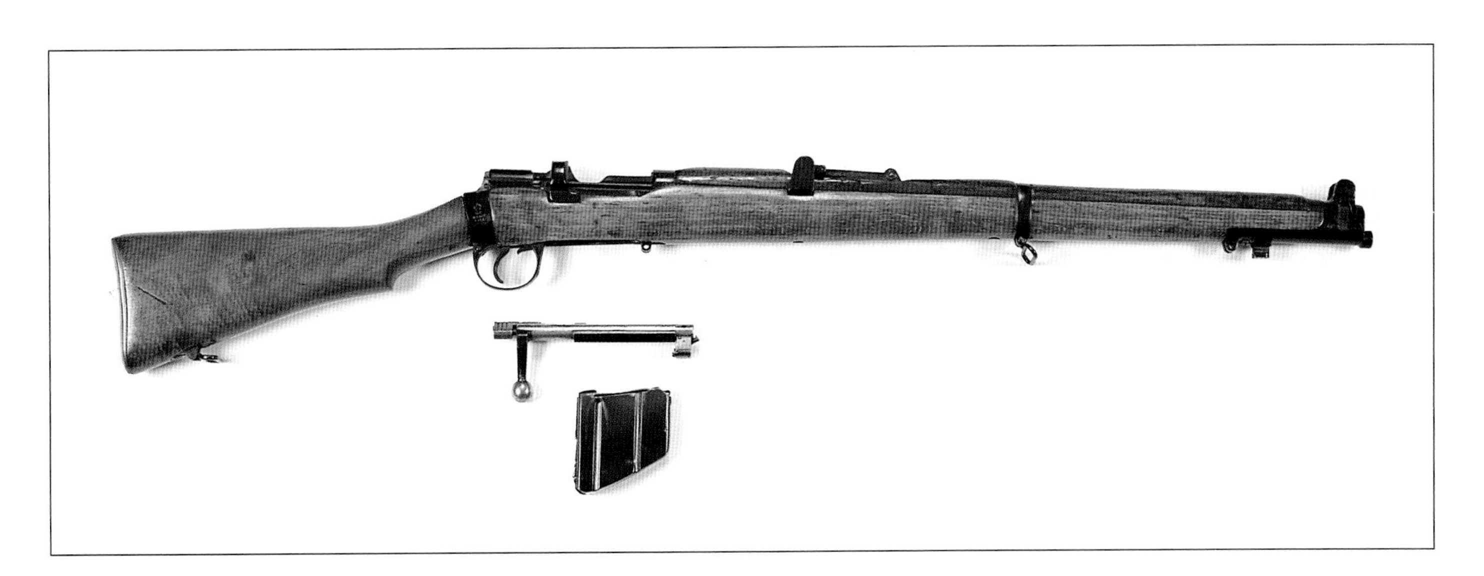

This field stripped SMLE illustrates all the working parts with which the soldier in the field is concerned when maintaining his weapon.

TYPE:	**7.65 MM LUGER PATTERN 08 PISTOL**
MANUFACTURER:	DWM (Erfurt and others)
DATE IN USE:	1908
COUNTRY OF MANUFACTURE:	Germany
OPERATION:	recoil action, semi-automatic
FEED:	8 round magazine
LENGTH:	8.5 in/216 mm
WEIGHT:	1.93 lb/0.88 kg
EFFECTIVE RANGE:	close quarters

The original version of the Luger pistol was built to take the 7.65 mm cartridge and was adopted as the service pistol for Switzerland in 1900. Later models standardised on 9 mm. In 1904 it was adopted as the standard pistol of the German Navy followed by the Army in 1908 and remained so until 1938. German production continued until 1943 and it continued to be widely used in a number of variations although superseded by the Walther P38. The Luger was a popular pistol but suffered from stoppages caused by dirt getting into the exposed action.

TYPE:	**9 MM LUGER PATTERN 08 PISTOL**
MANUFACTURER:	DWM (Erfurt and others)
DATE IN USE:	1940
COUNTRY OF MANUFACTURE:	Germany
OPERATION:	recoil action, semi-automatic
FEED:	8 round magazine
LENGTH:	8.5 in/216 mm (14.75 in/375 mm with silencer)
WEIGHT:	1.93 lb/.88 kg (2.7 lb/1.23 kg with silencer)
EFFECTIVE RANGE:	close quarters

Besides the German production, the Luger was manufactured by Switzerland and by Vickers in the UK for the Dutch Government. In total some 2,000,000 were built in at least 35 different versions.

This particular Luger was used by the British Special Operations Executive during World War Two and is fitted with a Maxim type silencer.

TYPE:	**9 MM LUGER MODEL 1917 'ARTILLERY' PISTOL**
MANUFACTURER:	DWM (Erfurt and others)
DATE IN USE:	1917
COUNTRY OF MANUFACTURE:	Germany
OPERATION:	recoil action, semi-automatic
FEED:	8 round magazine or 32 round drum magazine (illustrated)
LENGTH:	12.5 in/317 mm (25.75 in/654 mm as illustrated)
WEIGHT:	2.18 lb/0.99 kg (5.3 lb/2.41 kg as illustrated)
EFFECTIVE RANGE:	close quarters (sights 109 yd/100 m to 875 yd/800 m)

The Navy Luger and long barrelled Pattern 1908 Type pistols are similar in design. The Navy Luger is fitted with a 6 in (152 mm) barrel while the long barrelled 1908 (which is also referred to as the Model 1914, Model 1917 or Artillery) is fitted with an 8 in (203 mm) barrel. Both were fitted with a wooden shoulder stock which doubles as a holster while the 1908 was often issued with a 32 round 'Snail' magazine.

TYPE:	**.45 IN M1911A1**
MANUFACTURER:	Colt (Browning)
DATE IN USE:	1911
COUNTRY OF MANUFACTURE:	USA
OPERATION:	recoil, semi-automatic
FEED:	7 round magazine
LENGTH:	8.62 in/219 mm
WEIGHT:	2.43 lb/1.10 kg
EFFECTIVE RANGE:	close quarters

A .45 calibre pistol was designed by Browning in 1911 and the original manufacture was carried out by Colt. By 1914 Springfield had tooled up, but when the US entered World War One their manufacturing capacity was required for rifle production. By the end of the war some 450,000 Model 1911 pistols had been made, mainly by Colt, assisted by Remington. In 1926 modifications to the design resulted in new production being designated M1911A1.

During World War Two the Model 1911A1 continued to be manufactured by Colt together with Remington Rand, Union Switch and Signal and the Ithaca Gun Co with some 1,800,000 being built.

Altogether, approximately 2,400,000 of this .45 pistol have been built for the US Government in addition to licensed production in Japan as the Type 57 New Nambu and Argentina as the Pistola Sistema Colt 1927.

TYPE:	**7.63 MM MODEL 1912 SELF-LOADING PISTOL**
MANUFACTURER:	Mauser
DATE IN USE:	1912
COUNTRY OF MANUFACTURE:	Germany
OPERATION:	recoil action, semi-automatic
FEED:	10 or 20 round magazine
LENGTH:	11.5 lb/292 mm (24.8 in/630 mm with stock)
WEIGHT:	2.5 lb/1.14 kg (3.5 lb/1.59 kg with stock)
EFFECTIVE RANGE:	close quarters (sights to 1,094 yd/1,000 m)

The Model 1912 was developed from the original design of 1896. It introduced the six groove rifling and a safety catch which could be operated in the cocked or fired position. It also featured a revised hammer head design.

In 1916 Mauser commenced construction of a 9 mm variant due to the German need to standardise ammunition requirements.

The Mauser Model 1912 is shown fitted with the wooden holster being used as stock. Without this fitted, the pistol was difficult to fire accurately and tended to shoot high.

TYPE: **7.63 MM MODEL 1912 SELF-LOADING PISTOL**

The Model 1912 complete with wooden butt/holster and a clip of dummy cartridges.

TYPE:	**.30 IN BROWNING MACHINE OR AUTOMATIC RIFLE (BAR)**
MANUFACTURER:	Winchester (Colt and others)
DATE IN USE:	1918
COUNTRY OF MANUFACTURE:	USA
OPERATION:	gas operated, automatic
FEED:	20 round magazine
LENGTH:	46.25 in/1,175 mm
WEIGHT:	15.5 lb/7.04 kg
EFFECTIVE RANGE:	600 yd/550 m (sights 200 yd/183 m to 1,600 yd/1,462 m)

Browning originally conceived the .30 Browning Automatic Rifle (BAR) at the turn of the century. However, due to US Government lack of interest, he continued to develop and market pistols, shotguns and hunting rifles, for which there was a large commercial market.

In 1917 a presentation of the BAR was arranged before some 300 guests from US and foreign armed forces. The various demonstrations showed the operation of the BAR including semi- and fully automatic fire – a 20 round magazine was emptied in just two and a half seconds!

The BAR was pushed into rapid production, manufactured by Colt, Winchester and Marlin Rockwell. The US Army 79th Division was the first to take this rifle into France when it landed in 1918. It was first used in action that September. Despite the American enthusiasm for the BAR, this was not felt universally. It was widely considered to be too heavy for an automatic rifle but too light to deliver effective full automatic fire.

The BAR was also built by FN for Belgium, Chile and China.

TYPE:	**.303 (BROWNING) AUTOMATIC RIFLE**
MANUFACTURER:	Colt (Winchester and others)
DATE IN USE:	1918
COUNTRY OF MANUFACTURE:	USA
OPERATION:	gas, selective
FEED:	20 round magazine
LENGTH:	43.4 in/1,100 mm
WEIGHT:	18.19 lb/8.25 kg
EFFECTIVE RANGE:	600 yd/550 m (sights 200 yd/183 m to 1,300 yd/1,188 m)

The Browning .303 Automatic Rifle (referred to as the .30-06 Automatic Machine Rifle in the US) was developed by John Browning for US use in World War One.

Four basic US versions were produced and some 85,000 of the Model 1918 were built by Colt, Winchester and Rockwell during World War One. Model 1918A was adopted in 1937 and is similar to the M1918 with the addition of a hinged shoulder support plate on the butt and a supporting spiked bipod just forward of the forearm attached to the gas cylinder. This resulted in an increase in weapon weight which continued with subsequent models.

The Model 1918A2 came into service in 1937 and was initially made by converting Model 1918 and 1918A1s. On this model, the bipod, which was fitted with skids replacing the spikes, had moved forward and located on the flash muzzle. A second support in the form of a removable stock rest was also issued initially. The forearm was further reduced in height and made shorter, and there was a shorter shoulder rest. It also had magazine guards fitted on the trigger guard. It has a sight fitted which has micrometer adjustment for windage as well as elevation.

The Model 1922 was short-lived having been designed to give the horse cavalry of the 1920s increased firepower. The barrel has radial cooling fins and a groove around the butt/stock for a rest clamp. This variant was obsolete prior to the US entering World War Two.

A further model was introduced in 1949 which was the T34 Automatic Rifle and developed to take the NATO 7.62 mm ammunition. Colt continued to manufacture this as the Monitor and R75A.

TYPE:	**13 MM T GEWEHR**
MANUFACTURER:	Mauser
DATE IN USE:	1918
COUNTRY OF MANUFACTURE:	Germany
OPERATION:	bolt action, single shot
LENGTH:	66.75 in/1,695 mm
WEIGHT:	38 lb/17.25 kg
EFFECTIVE RANGE:	109 yd/100 m (sights 109 yd/100 m to 547 yd/500 m)

The early British tanks could be damaged by ordinary rifle and machine gun fire, but in June 1917 the first Mark IV tanks appeared.These were armoured to withstand the ordinary lead bullets and the toughened 'K' type bullets.

When the Germans realised this they immediately instigated a programme to develop a new weapon. The result was the T Gewehr which was the first anti-tank rifle of World War One.

The T Gewehr was a scaled-up 7.92 mm calibre Model 98 rifle firing the specially manufactured 13 mm ammunition. Although it was capable of penetrating a Mark IV tank at 120 yd (110 m), this could only be achieved when fired at right angles to the tank. At 45 degrees and at 60 yd (55 m) it was incapable of penetrating even the thinnest plate.

TYPE:	**7.65 MM PP PISTOL**
MANUFACTURER:	Walther
DATE IN USE:	1929
COUNTRY OF MANUFACTURE:	Germany
OPERATION:	blowback
FEED:	8 round magazine
LENGTH:	6.7 in/170 mm
WEIGHT:	1.63 lb/0.74 kg
EFFECTIVE RANGE:	close quarters

The 7.65 mm Model PP (Polizei Pistole) was originally made for police from 1929 but later used by the German army during World War Two.

The original version was of 7.65 calibre but subsequent variants have been built for .22 in, 6.35 mm and 9 mm Short. The Hungarian PA-63 and Model AP is based on the PP. The PP is still in production and has been widely issued to armed forces, police and government agencies. In the British service it was known as the L47E1.

TYPE:	**7.65 MM PPK AUTOMATIC PISTOL**
MANUFACTURER:	Walther
DATE IN USE:	1931
COUNTRY OF MANUFACTURE:	Germany
OPERATION:	blowback, double-action
FEED:	7 round magazine
LENGTH:	6.25 in/159 mm
WEIGHT:	1.61 lb/0.73 kg
EFFECTIVE RANGE:	close quarters

The 7.65 PPK (Polizei Pistole Kriminal) was originally produced for detectives but, like the longer PP, it was widely used by the German Army during World War Two. Pre-war production PPKs were fitted with a pin which protruded when the chamber was loaded, although this was often omitted during wartime production when the quality of finish was usually lower. Like the PP, the PPK was originally designed for the 7.65 mm cartridge but later versions were built to accommodate the .22, 6.35 mm and 9 mm ammunition.

It has been made under licence in France, Hungary and Turkey. It has widespread use by the German and other European armed forces as well as police and government agencies.

TYPE:	**.38 IN NO.2 MK.1* REVOLVER**
MANUFACTURER:	Enfield (Webley)
DATE IN USE:	1932
COUNTRY OF MANUFACTURE:	UK
OPERATION:	double-action
FEED:	6 round cylinder
LENGTH:	10 in/254 mm
WEIGHT:	1.3 lb/0.59 kg
EFFECTIVE RANGE:	close quarters

The Revolver No.2 was designed and built by Enfield in the late 1920s and was subsequently introduced into British service. This No.2 Mk.1 was built by Albion Motors who built in excess of 40,000 as a wartime expedient.

TYPE:	**8 MM TYPE 94 AUTOMATIC PISTOL**
MANUFACTURER:	not known
DATE IN USE:	1934
COUNTRY OF MANUFACTURE:	Japan
OPERATION:	recoil-operated, semi-automatic
FEED:	6 round magazine
LENGTH:	7.2 in/183 mm
WEIGHT:	1.8 lb/0.82 kg
EFFECTIVE RANGE:	close quarters

This 8 mm pistol was introduced in 1934 to target the export market initially. It was used as a service pistol during World War Two by the Japanese as the Type 94.

TYPE:	**9 MM BELGIUM BROWNING PISTOL**
MANUFACTURER:	Fabrique Nationale Herstal (FN)
DATE IN USE:	1935
COUNTRY OF MANUFACTURE:	Belgium
OPERATION:	recoil-operated, semi-automatic
FEED:	13 round magazine
LENGTH:	7.75 lb/197 mm
WEIGHT:	2 lb/0.91 kg
EFFECTIVE RANGE:	close quarters (sights to 500 yd/457 m)

The Browning High Power pistol was the last model developed by John Browning before he died in 1926. Although the prototypes existed in 1926, the pistol was not marketed until 1935. Since then this 9 mm pistol has become one of the most widely used pistols in the world.

As well as being used by the Belgian forces during World War Two, the pistol was manufactured in occupied Liege for the German SS troops as the Pistole 640 and by the John Inglis Company of Canada for the Australian, Canadian and Chinese armies. It was also used by British Commandos, Paratroops and Special Forces during World War Two. Also, further supplies were made to Denmark (Pistol M/46), Netherlands (Pistol, 9 mm Browning), Lithuania and Romania with licensed production in Indonesia as the Pindad PiA 9 mm.

The 9 mm Browning is still in production by FN Nouvelle Herstal and it is widely used by many Western nations as well as by the Belgian Forces.

TYPE:	**7.65 MM M1935A PISTOL**
MANUFACTURER:	not known
DATE IN USE:	1935
COUNTRY OF MANUFACTURE:	France
OPERATION:	recoil-operated, semi-automatic
FEED:	8 round magazine
LENGTH:	8.63 in/219 mm
WEIGHT:	1.75 lb/0.79 kg
EFFECTIVE RANGE:	close quarters

The M1935A was the standard pistol of the French Army in World War Two. It is externally similar to the Model 1935S which has a different locking system. It is based on the patent of C. Petter of SACM and is a modification of the Browning recoil-operated pistols. They were built by a number of French small arms manufacturers including Saint Etienne (MAS).

The type of ammunition used was the same as used in the Pedersan device, although this ammunition was not considered to be particularly effective.

The French armed forces continued to use the M1935A after World War Two, during the conflict in Indo-China until 1954.

TYPE:	**.30-06 IN M1 GARAND RIFLE**
MANUFACTURER:	Springfield
DATE IN USE:	1936
COUNTRY OF MANUFACTURE:	USA
OPERATION:	gas, semi-automatic
FEED:	8 round clip
LENGTH:	43 in/1,092 mm
WEIGHT:	9.4 lb/4.26 kg
EFFECTIVE RANGE:	984 yd/900 m (sights 200 yd/183 m to 1,200 yd1,097 m)

The M1 Garand was the first self-loading rifle to be adopted in quantity for military service and replaced the Model 1903A1 in US service. During 1939 deliveries were slow, but by the end of 1945 over 4,000,000 had been built.

Production continued in the US during the Korean War with a further 500,000 being built. In addition, outside the US, a production line was set up by Pietro Beretta in Italy who built over 100,000 examples for the Italian, Danish and Indonesian armed forces. Many were converted into different variants, including the Italian 7.62 mm BM series, which was the best known.

US production was by Springfield Armoury (Government), Harrington and Richardson and International Harvester. In 1974 Springfield Armoury Inc acquired the rights to the Springfield Armoury from the US Government and the M1 Garand remained in production for commercial sales. Production has now been terminated, although spares and service remain available. The M1D, which is fitted with the M84 telescope, remains in service as a sniper rifle.

About some 6,000,000 examples of the M1 Garand were built, and this rifle has been used by the US Army, US National Guard, Brazil, Chile, Costa Rica, Denmark, Greece, Guatemala, Haiti, Honduras, Indonesia, Italy, Philippines, Taiwan, Tunisia, Turkey and UK.

TYPE:	**7.62 MM TT-33 (TULA TOKAREV) SELF-LOADING PISTOL**
MANUFACTURER:	Tokarev
DATE IN USE:	1938
COUNTRY OF MANUFACTURE:	USSR
OPERATION:	recoil-operated, semi-automatic
FEED:	8 round magazine
LENGTH:	7.65 in/194 mm
WEIGHT:	2 lb/0.91 kg
EFFECTIVE RANGE:	close quarters

The Tokarev TT-33 was developed from the Tokarev M1930 pistol which was itself derived from the Browning designed Colt M1911. Parts of the design were simplified or modified by Tokarev, especially the lock mechanism, magazine and safety arrangements.

Soviet production of the TT-33 ceased in 1954, although it is still in production in Hungary as the Model 48 and the former Yugoslavia as the 7.62 mm M57 and 9 mm M70 and probably continues elsewhere. It was used widely within the old Warsaw Pact countries and China as the Type 51 as well as by many guerrilla forces.

TYPE:	**9 MM P38 AUTOMATIC PISTOL**
MANUFACTURER:	Walther
DATE IN USE:	1938
COUNTRY OF MANUFACTURE:	Germany
OPERATION:	recoil-operated, semi-automatic
FEED:	8 round magazine
LENGTH:	8.34 in/212 mm
WEIGHT:	2.1 lb/0.95 kg
EFFECTIVE RANGE:	close quarters

The P38 was adopted for the German Army in 1938 and by the end of World War Two over 1,000,000 of this pistol had been built. Various versions were produced including the P38 with a 5 in barrel, P4 with 4.5 in barrel and P38K with 2.75 in barrel.

The P38 is still in production as the P1, which is used by the Chilean, Norwegian, Portuguese and German armed forces amongst others.

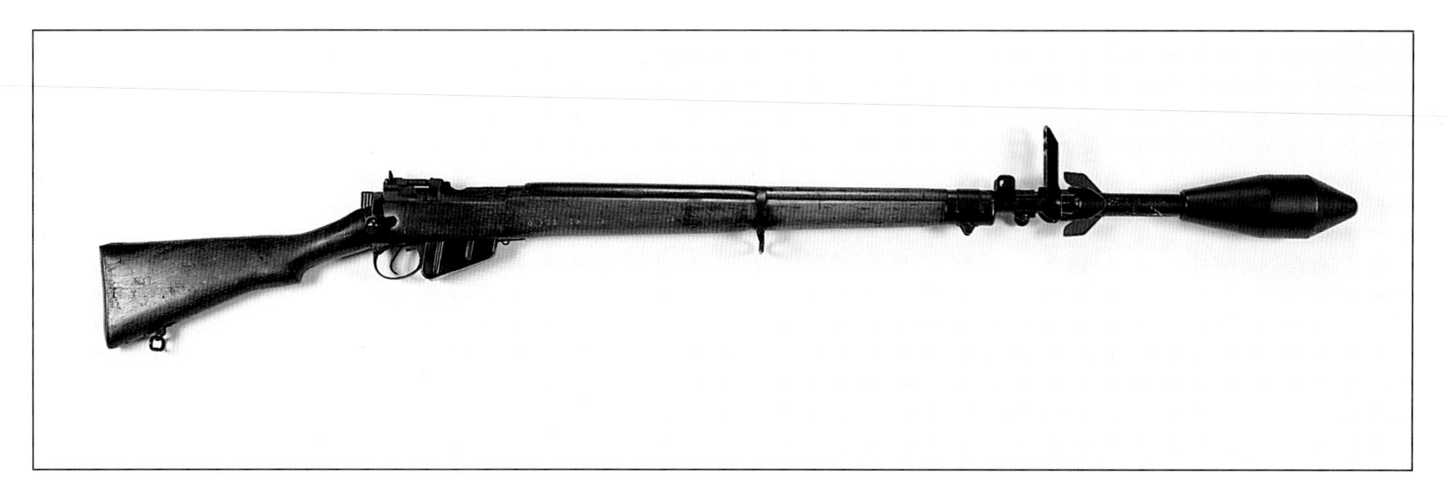

TYPE:	**.303 IN NO.4 MK.I RIFLE**
MANUFACTURER:	Enfield
DATE IN USE:	1939
COUNTRY OF MANUFACTURE:	UK
OPERATION:	bolt action
FEED:	10 round magazine
LENGTH:	43.75 in/1,111 mm
WEIGHT:	8.5 lb/3.86 kg
EFFECTIVE RANGE:	547 yd/500 m (sights to 1,300 yd/1422 m)

The Enfield No.4 rifle resulted from trials of an improved No.1 rifle. An initial batch was built in 1931 with an aperture sight, heavier barrel and lighter bayonet. It was simpler to manufacture than the Mk.1 and required less machining, but due to the large availability of surplus Mk.1 variants from World War One available for repair and upgrade, new rifle production did not proceed.

Following the outbreak of World War Two production commenced at two new Royal Ordnance Factories – Maltby and Fazakerly, and at BSA in Shirley. In addition production commenced in the US and Canada. By the end of the war over 2,000,000 No.4 rifles had been built in the UK and 5,000,000 worldwide. This No.4 rifle is fitted with spigot discharger and a No.94 anti-tank training grenade.

TYPE:	**.55 IN BOYS MK.1 ANTI-TANK RIFLE**
MANUFACTURER:	Enfield
DATE IN USE:	1939
COUNTRY OF MANUFACTURE:	UK
OPERATION:	bolt action
FEED:	5 round magazine
LENGTH:	63.25 in/1,606 mm
WEIGHT:	38 lb/17.25 kg
EFFECTIVE RANGE:	not applicable

The Boys Anti-tank Rifle was mainly the result of the design work carried out by Capt Boys – Assistant Superintendent of Design at Enfield in the 1930s. This rifle was developed to satisfy a requirement for an anti-armour weapon.

Two main variants of the Boys Anti-Tank Rifle were constructed – the Mk.1 & Mk.1* – although some sub-variants were also built. Nearly 100,000 Boys were built by BSA in the UK together with US and Canadian production.

This type of weapon depends on high velocity combined with a hardened bullet to achieve penetration. Improvements in armour rendered most anti-tank rifles ineffective including the Boys. Explosive, and in particular, hollow charge missiles took over in this role.

TYPE:	**7.65 MM MODEL 27 PISTOL**
MANUFACTURER:	Brohmische Waffenfabrik (Ceska Zbrojovka)
DATE IN USE:	1939
COUNTRY OF MANUFACTURE:	Czechoslovakia
OPERATION:	blowback, semi-automatic
FEED:	8 round magazine
LENGTH:	6.3 in/160 mm
WEIGHT:	1.56 lb/0.71 kg
EFFECTIVE RANGE:	close quarters

The Model 27 was originally built by Ceska Zbrojovka (CZ) of Prague. Production continued after the occupation by German forces at the beginning of World War Two, when the name of the factory was changed to Brohmische Waffenfabrik AG, and those manufactured during the war are stamped 'fnh'. The factory reverted back to the original CZ once the war was over.

In 1948 the name changed once more, following the Communist take-over, when 'Narodni Podnik' (People's Factory) was added. Production of the Model 27 continued until the early 1950s and achieved the greatest production of all pre-war Czech pistols.

This example was manufactured during German occupation.

TYPE:	**.303 IN NO.4 MK.I(T) RIFLE**
MANUFACTURER:	Lee Enfield
DATE IN USE:	1942
COUNTRY OF MANUFACTURE:	UK
OPERATION:	bolt action
FEED:	10 round magazine
LENGTH:	43.75 in/1,111 mm
WEIGHT:	11.6 lb/5.26 kg
EFFECTIVE RANGE:	437 yd/400 m (sights to 1,000 yd/914 m)

The No.4 Mk.I(T) sniper rifle became the standard British sniper rifle from 1943 onwards. Nearly 28,000 of this variant were specially selected for high accuracy during test and then modified from the standard Mk.4 with a cheek pad and a No.32 sight added.

TYPE:	**7.62 MM SVT-40 SELF-LOADING RIFLE**
MANUFACTURER:	Tokarev
DATE IN USE:	1940
COUNTRY OF MANUFACTURE:	USSR
OPERATION:	gas, semi-automatic
FEED:	10 round magazine
LENGTH:	47.5 in/1,206 mm
WEIGHT:	8.5 lb/3.86 kg
EFFECTIVE RANGE:	1,094 yd/1,000 m (sights 109 yd/100 m to 1,640 yd/1,500 m)

The Tokarev first emerged as a development of the Simonov in 1938 with a modified version in 1940. It was too light in construction and therefore was not as useful. However, it was used effectively against the Germans by the Russians on the Eastern Front.

Production totalling 1,322,085 SVT-40 plus 51,710 SVT-40 sniper version were built by Soviet weapons factories during World War Two.

TYPE:	**.32 IN ACP WELLROD PISTOL WITH INTEGRAL SILENCER**
MANUFACTURER:	Welwyn Garden
DATE IN USE:	1940
COUNTRY OF MANUFACTURE:	UK
OPERATION:	bolt action, single shot
LENGTH:	12 in/305 mm
WEIGHT:	2.6 lb/1.18 kg
EFFECTIVE RANGE:	close quarters

The Wellrod was officially designated the Mark I Hand Firing Device and used by the British Special Operations Executive during World War Two. It was also built in 7.65 mm and 9 mm calibres.

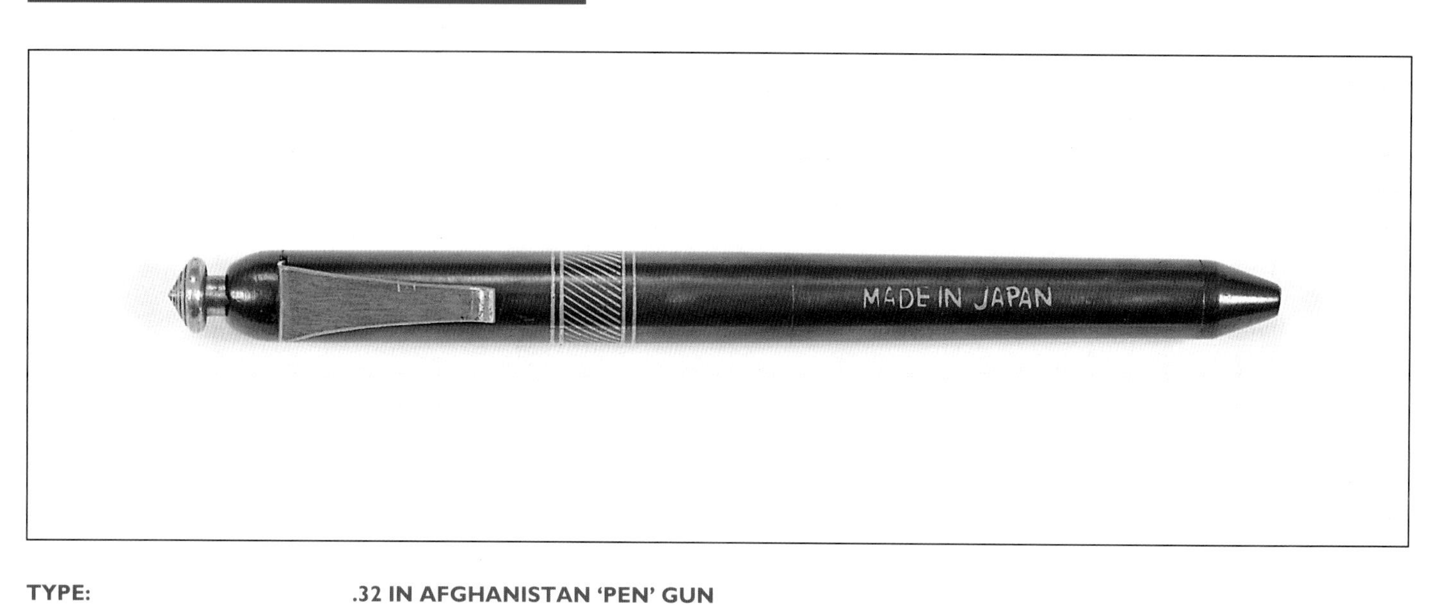

TYPE:	**.32 IN AFGHANISTAN 'PEN' GUN**
MANUFACTURER:	not known
DATE IN USE:	1940
COUNTRY OF MANUFACTURE:	stamped 'Japan'
OPERATION:	spring plunger
LENGTH:	5.3 in/135 mm
WEIGHT:	0.3 lb/0.14 kg
EFFECTIVE RANGE:	close quarters

This is basically a zip gun which has been well made and could easily pass as a pen.

The zip gun is an improvised weapon used to fire a cartridge. A large number are highly dangerous as they are homemade from materials not designed to stand the stresses caused by the explosion. The British Special Operations Executive produced a range of pen guns during World War Two and this is a typical example of this type of weapon.

TYPE:	**7.92 MM FG.42 PARATROOP RIFLE**
MANUFACTURER:	Rheinmettal-Borsig
DATE IN USE:	1942
COUNTRY OF MANUFACTURE:	Germany
OPERATION:	gas, selective fire
FEED:	20 round magazine
LENGTH:	38.25 in/1,010 mm
WEIGHT:	12 lb/5.45 kg
EFFECTIVE RANGE:	sights 109 yd/100 m to 1,312 yd/1,200 m

The Fallschirmjaeger Gewehr (Paratrooper Rifle) FG.42 was unusual in that it was developed at the request of the Luftwaffe for a selective fire weapon for paratroop use. This was as a result of the fact that the Luftwaffe controlled the airborne divisions, which had suffered disastrously during landings in Crete due to the lack of a suitable weapon. The FG.42 was to fulfil the role of rifle, light machine gun and sub-machine gun which it did successfully although it was not adopted by the German Army.

TYPE:	**1 IN SIGNAL PISTOL NO.1 MK.5 (VERY)**
MANUFACTURER:	I L Berridge
DATE IN USE:	1942
COUNTRY OF MANUFACTURE:	UK
OPERATION:	cartridge
LENGTH:	9.5 in/241 mm
WEIGHT:	1.94 lb/0.88 kg
EFFECTIVE RANGE:	not applicable

The use of pistols to send signals dates back to the 19th century. In the 1880s the introduction of the Very signal cartridge saw the design of a specialist signal pistol. Initially the signalling pistol was adopted by the Navy but was widely used by the outbreak of World War One. This particular signalling pistol was designated the No.1 Mk.5 – nearly 500,000 of these signal pistols were built during World War Two.

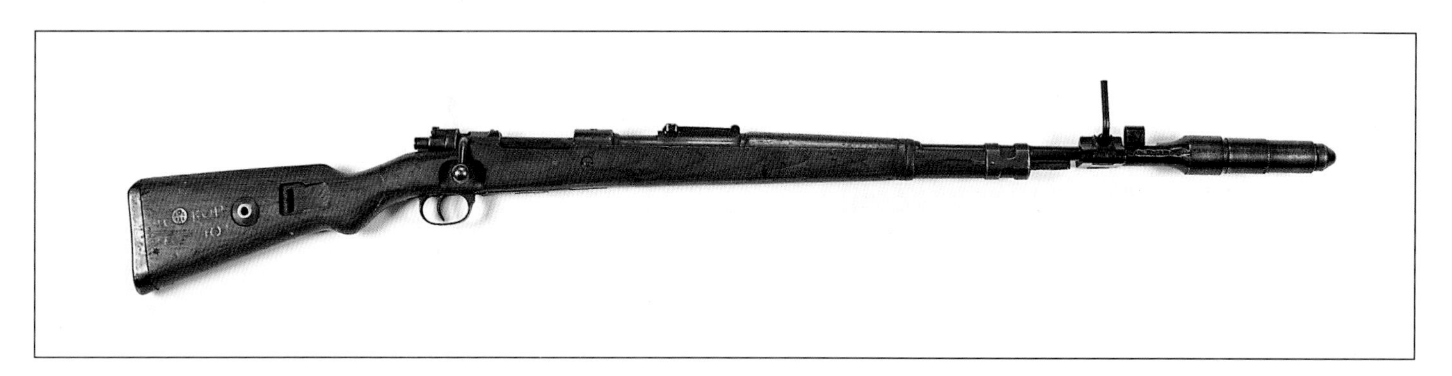

TYPE:	**7.92 MM MODEL KAR98K RIFLE**
MANUFACTURER:	Mauser
DATE IN USE:	1943
COUNTRY OF MANUFACTURE:	Germany
OPERATION:	bolt action
LENGTH:	43 in/1,092 mm
WEIGHT:	8.9 lb/4.04 kg
EFFECTIVE RANGE:	437 yd/400 m (sights 109 yd/100 m to 2,187yd/2,000 m)

Although Mauser had developed a semi-automatic rifle back in 1898, this type of weapon was not adopted by the Germans during World War One and only served in small quantities. Prior to World War Two Walther developed another semi-automatic, but the authorities preferred a modified Mauser Model 98 instead. The Model 98K ('K' means 'kurz' or short) was produced in large numbers throughout the war and it became the most widely used standard rifle. It was only in 1944 that the Germans began to replace the bolt action and existing semi-automatic rifles with a selective fire assault weapon.

This Mauser 98K is fitted with an anti-tank grenade incorporating a small bursting hollow charge. The maximum range of the grenade was 65 m.

Variants of the 98 action were built by FN in Belgium from 1924 until 1964 and with Zbrojovka Brno Czechoslovakia jointly from 1924–38.

During World War Two Belgium was occupied and various weapons continued to be manufactured under German control although the finished quality was not to the pre- or post-war standards.

TYPE:	**.30 IN RIFLE M1903A4**
MANUFACTURER:	Remington
DATE IN USE:	1943
COUNTRY OF MANUFACTURE:	USA
OPERATION:	manual bolt action
FEED:	5 round non-removable magazine
LENGTH:	43.2 in/1,097 mm
WEIGHT:	9.55 lb/4.34 kg
EFFECTIVE RANGE:	984 yd/900 m (sights 500 yd/457 m to 1,000 yd/914 m)

The Springfield M1903 was a US adaption of the German Mauser 98 and was used by the US Army during World War One. The A1 version introduced a few minor changes in 1929 of which the most visible was the pistol grip type of stock. The A2 variant was the result of an alteration to allow the removal of the bolt and instantly replaced it with the Pedersen device. This altered the rifle from bolt action to a blowback automatic. These were followed by a series of sports and competition rifles.

During World War Two the British Government contracted Remington to supply quantities of the M1903 in a desperate need to replace rifles lost at Dunkirk and as a result of reduced production due to enemy bombing.

In 1942 the M1903A4 was adopted for use as a sniper rifle. This M1903A4 (illustrated) is the sniper version of this Springfield rifle and is fitted with a Weaver 330C Scope or M73B1 x 2.5 sight. Due to the position of the scope this model can only be loaded with single cartridges and it is sighted to 1,200 yd (1,097 m). It was gradually replaced by the M1C and M1D Garand.

TYPE:	**7.92 MM KARBINER 43**
MANUFACTURER:	Walther
DATE IN USE:	1943
COUNTRY OF MANUFACTURE:	Germany
OPERATION:	gas, semi-automatic
LENGTH:	43.4 in/1,102 mm
WEIGHT:	10.5 lb/4.77 kg
EFFECTIVE RANGE:	437 yd/400 m (sights 91 yd/100 m to 876 yd/800 m)

The Karbiner 43 (Kar43) is basically similar to the Gewehr 43 (G43). It contains a mechanism which is the result of combining the bolt assembly of the G41W with a gas system designed by Walther. The Kar43 and G43 were built in substantial quantities and in many variations.

This second generation SLR is equipped with a ZF-4 x4 telescopic sight.

TYPE:	**7.92 MM (SHORT) MP.44 ASSAULT RIFLE**
MANUFACTURER:	Haenel, Mauser or Erma
DATE IN USE:	1944
COUNTRY OF MANUFACTURE:	Germany
OPERATION:	gas, selective fire
FEED:	30 round magazine
LENGTH:	36.6 in/930 mm
WEIGHT:	10.6 lb/4.81 kg
EFFECTIVE RANGE:	328 yd/300 m (sights 109 yd/100 m to 875 yd/800 m)

The MKb.42/MP.43/MP.44 family of weapons was significant in that it marked the initial adoption of an intermediate cartridge, selective assault rifle into large scale production. In 1943 the Mkb.42 was reworked and became the MP.43 and in early 1944 it was re-designated MP.44. Later that year it changed again, this time to Sturmgewehr 44 (StG.44) or Assault Rifle 44.

These assault rifles were supposed to replace the rifle, sub-machine gun and light machine gun for the infantry. Although production had reached 5,000 per month by February 1944, the war ended before significant quantities of rifles were delivered.

The MP.44 was the most advanced version of this series produced by the German design team during World War Two.

AUTOMATICS – A STEP FORWARD?

1945–1990

After World World One, the Treaty of Versailles stripped Germany of weaponry, so that when World War Two commenced, Germany set about re-equipping her supplies. Much emphasis was concentrated on building the general purpose machine gun and the sub-machine gun which were produced in substantial quantities. A modified version of the 1898 Mauser, the shorter Mauser 98K, had been selected as the rifle. Although German small arms were not attractive, they were easy to mass produce with much use of metal stampings and pressings used to replace time-consuming machining.

Production of the American semi-automatic M1 Garand was progressing slowly with some 50,000 in service by 1940. The British Army had stayed with the bolt action rifle, as had France, and were paying the price with insufficient firepower compared to the Germans who now had substantial quantities of machine guns and sub-machine guns. Production was quickly adjusted and the sub-machine gun and light machine gun rapidly gained importance.

The sub-machine gun was a useful weapon, but its design limited it to small ammunition, which meant that it lacked the range and hitting power. The Germans were the first to develop a replacement, when, in 1942, they produced their first light automatic weapon, later to be known as the assault rifle. This assault rifle could be handled like a rifle but could produce automatic fire. The problem with this early weapon was that the power of the full-sized cartridge was too much for a soldier to hold unsupported. When the problem was thought through, the answer lay in the actual use for this weapon. The standard rifle cartridge was capable of around 2,187 yd (2,000 m). The assault rifle was intended for use in a battle and only required a range of around 300 m. By reducing the power of the charge, an intermediate round could be produced, thus reducing the recoil. The result was the German MP44 assault rifle.

Until this stage, the most automated of firing mechanisms would be considered semi-automatic. However automatic the reloading, the semi-automatic weapon requires that the trigger is operated for every round fired. The introduction of the automatic weapon meant that on these guns the firing mechanism would repeat the firing sequence as long as the trigger remained pressed and ammunition remained. Although this was an advance, it was found to be extravagant to operate as large quantities of ammunition were expended – usually unnecessarily. The majority of modern automatic weapons have a switch which enables the soldier to adjust his weapon to 'selective fire' which enables a predetermined number of rounds to be automatically fired and requires the trigger to be released before any more rounds are fired. The forces imposed on an automatic weapon meant that it was difficult to fire accurately during a long burst and therefore ammunition was easily wasted. The 'selective fire' enables reasonable aim to be taken and reduces this wastage.

During the 1920s and early 1930s there was a general reluctance to replace existing weaponry due to the costs involved. As a result, the British Army still had the .455 in Webley revolvers in general use after World War One due to the widespread shortage of any other side arms. However, a similar design was under construction by Enfield in .38 in calibre. Additional production for the British was carried out by Smith & Wesson, as well as Colt, whose .38 in revolvers could easily be modified to take the newly introduced standard of .38 in pistol ammunition.

The American services still had stocks of their World War One Smith & Wesson as well as Colt .45 in revolvers but large quantities of the .38 in calibre revolvers were being built. Russia, on the other hand, had some revolvers but decided that production of sub-machine guns would be more effective in terms of cost and firepower available.

A number of specialist small arms were produced during World War Two such as the Welrod. This bolt action, single shot pistol was silenced for use by Special Forces.

The British saw no need for anti-tank weapons in World War One as the Germans only managed to produce a limited number of tanks towards the end of the war. When it became obvious that Germany was re-arming, designs of a suitable weapon were prepared and resulted in the Boys anti-tank rifle. Although produced in reasonable numbers the day of the anti-tank rifle was over due to improvements in tank armour, and it was subsequently replaced by various missile systems.

The value of the pistol or revolver as a military weapon continues to be debated. An American study has questioned their role in a modern conflict. However, the psychological value of the reassurance provided by such weapons as a means of defence for the individual should not be underestimated.

For British Commandos the 9 mm Browning pistol with its 13 round magazines had proved to be a valuable weapon, but then these were being used by well trained troops. On the Eastern front the Russians had already decided not to issue pistols and had provided sub-machine guns and machine guns instead as they were cheaper and more effective. Although the Germans were initially strong believers in automatic pistols for officers and some other groups of soldiers, as the war progressed they were reaching the same conclusions as the Russians.

At the end of the war the Soviets produced what was to become one of the most famous of all assault rifles – the Kalashnikov AK47. Subsequently built by many communist countries, they have found their way into the hands of many terrorist groups.

The numbers of assault rifles have grown from strength to strength since World War Two. A major subject for discussion has been and still is the calibre of the bullet. NATO has always tried to maintain a standard ammunition even though there have been a variety of different weapons using it. The crux of the problem has always been to get the right balance of ammunition that will fire a bullet over a required range, be powerful enough to stop the advancing enemy yet be light enough to enable a soldier to carry a sufficient quantity of rounds.

During World War Two, the Germans used 7.92 mm ammunition, while the British had .303 in and the Americans .30 in. Soon after the end of the war Britain was keen to have an assault rifle to replace the old bold action Enfield No.4 rifle. The design chosen was the .28 in calibre EM2 assault rifle which proved to be effective. However, NATO and especially the US, who had huge stocks of existing .30 in ammunition, did not want to make the change, so, under pressure, Britain adopted the Belgian 7.62 mm FN rifle which was subsequently designated L1A1 in the British Army.

During the 1970s the operational commitments of the British Army changed and it was therefore felt that the L1A1 was too long and that an assault rifle was desperately needed. The debate commenced once again with Britain deciding on a 4.85 mm calibre weapon for the next generation known as the XL65 or Individual Weapon. Examples were built and tested and found to be highly effective. Britain was overruled once more with the NATO decision to follow the American lead of 5.56 mm calibre. While the Americans continued to use their M16s Britain developed the 5.56 mm SA80 Individual Weapon. Although this debate has subsided for the moment, the discussion still continues.

Despite the steady movement away from pistols and revolvers towards the sub-machine gun, they still remain very much part of the military hardware. Although it is accepted that they can play a limited role in any offensive action, they do provide a means of self defence for those personnel whose duties mean that a larger weapon would be impractical. This includes most officers, security personnel and others such as tank crews. Without a revolver or pistol they would be required to proceed into the battle area unarmed which would place them at a distinct psychological disadvantage.

This has ensured that some of the early classic small arms such as the 1911 Pistol, PP, PPK and P38 pistols remain in production much as they were when first produced. Development of new automatic pistols continues, but at a slow rate. The new weapons take advantage of new materials such as alloys or plastics to reduce weight or to improve handling.

The rifle is in a downward trend for the infantry soldier who is more likely to be equipped with an assault rifle or possibly a sub-machine gun. Virtually the only new rifles are for the specialist troops such as the snipers who are required to be able to place a single bullet onto the target. For this they are likely to be issued with a specialist rifle such as the Dragunov or the Accuracy International L96 and fitted with a powerful telescopic sight. The sniper will be supplied with specially selected ammunition and will hide away for periods of time, often heavily camouflaged to await his target.

TYPE:	**7.62 MM SKS 45 SIMONOV SEMI-AUTOMATIC CARBINE**
MANUFACTURER:	State factories
DATE IN USE:	1945
COUNTRY OF MANUFACTURE:	USSR
OPERATION:	gas, semi-automatic only
FEED:	10 round magazine
LENGTH:	39.75 in/1,010 mm
WEIGHT:	7.75 lb/3.52 kg
EFFECTIVE RANGE:	437 yd/400 m (sights to 1,094 yd/1,000 m)

The SKS is often considered to be a smaller version of the 14.5 mm PTRS semi-automatic anti-tank rifle of World War Two. It has a light recoil and is capable of firing accurately at 35 rounds per minute.

The SKS has an integral blade type bayonet which is kept folded back under the barrel when not required. The SKS was built in China as the Type 56 and North Korea as the Type 63, East Germany as Karbiner S and Yugoslavia as the M59/66. The SKS is now obsolete in the CIS having been replaced by the AK-47 although, it is still used in some Asian countries.

TYPE:	**7.62 MM TYPE 56 CARBINE**
MANUFACTURER:	State factories
DATE IN USE:	1945
COUNTRY OF MANUFACTURE:	China (USSR)

The Type 56 is the Chinese built version of the Soviet SKS 45. Although very similar there are a few differences such as the spike type bayonet.

This particular Type 56 was captured in Cambodia.

TYPE:	**.30 IN CRISTOBAL MODEL II AUTOMATIC CARBINE**
MANUFACTURER:	Armeria en San Cristobal
DATE IN USE:	1948
COUNTRY OF MANUFACTURE:	Dominican Republic
OPERATION:	delayed blowback, selective fire
FEED:	25 or 30 round magazine
LENGTH:	37.2 in/945 mm
WEIGHT:	7.75 lb/3.5 kg
EFFECTIVE RANGE:	350 yd/320 m

An unusual delayed blowback, selective fire Carbine designed for the US .30 in Carbine ammunition. The manufacturing facility was established with technical assistance from Beretta and Hungary. As a result the Model 2 bears a close resemblance to Beretta designs.

TYPE:	**7.62 MM (SHORT) AK-47 ASSAULT RIFLE**
MANUFACTURER:	Kalashnikov
DATE IN USE:	1949
COUNTRY OF MANUFACTURE:	USSR
OPERATION:	gas, selective fire
FEED:	30 round magazine
LENGTH:	33.9 in/861 mm
WEIGHT:	8 lb/3.63 kg
EFFECTIVE RANGE:	328 yd/300 m (sights to 219 yd/200 m and 875 yd/800 m)

The AK (Automat Kalashnikov) was designed in about 1947 and replaced the SKS. Subsequently referred to as the AK-47, this was to become the standard weapon of the Soviet Army from the early 1950s. It was later issued to CIS Navy and Air Force ground troops. In addition it was adopted as the weapon for all members of what was the Warsaw Pact as well as most of the other communist and former-communist countries. It has also been made available to many terrorist groups.

In addition to the Soviet manufacture, the AK-47 has been built in a number of the Warsaw Pact arsenals: in the former East Germany as the MPiK; in Finland as the M60, M62 and M76; Poland as the DGN-60; and China as the Type 56. Probably in excess of 20,000,000 AK-47s have been built.

This has been the most prolific rifle in service since World War Two.

TYPE:	**7.62 MM (SHORT) AK-47 ASSAULT RIFLE**

Field stripped example of the AK-47 showing the increasing complexity of components.

TYPE:	**.30 IN/7.62 MM EM2 RIFLE**
MANUFACTURER:	Enfield
DATE IN USE:	1949
COUNTRY OF MANUFACTURE:	UK
OPERATION:	gas
FEED:	20 round magazine
LENGTH:	34.5 in/876 mm
WEIGHT:	8.13 lb/3.69 kg
EFFECTIVE RANGE:	383 yd/350 m (sights to 600 yd/548 m)

The EM2 was a bullpup design by Stefan Janson of Royal Ordnance at Enfield Lock for the British developed intermediate .280 in (7 mm) cartridge. In 1949 the .280 mm ammunition was about to be adopted as standard for the British Army when a NATO standardisation meeting halted any further progress. Eventually the British Government relented in the face of overwhelming opposition to accept the US 7.62 mm ammunition.

This particular EM2 was re-barrelled to take the 7.62 mm ammunition. Unfortunately, the timescale for thorough re-design and testing was unacceptable in view of the already available and proved FN and orders for the FN were placed in 1957 by the British.

TYPE:	**7.62 MM FAL RIFLE**
MANUFACTURER:	Fabrica Militar de Armas Portatiles
DATE IN USE:	1950
COUNTRY OF MANUFACTURE:	Argentina (Belgium)
OPERATION:	gas, selective or semi-automatic fire
FEED:	20 round magazine
LENGTH:	43 in/1,092 mm
WEIGHT:	10.2 lb/4.63 kg
EFFECTIVE RANGE:	328 yd/300 m (sights to 656 yd/600 m)

The FN FAL is the result of a modified and improved version of the earlier FN semi-automatic rifle. It has also been widely produced for many other armed forces of the West. Licensed manufacture has been conducted in Argentina, Australia (L1A1), Austria (StG 58), Canada (C1) and India (L1A1)

Illustrated is a FAL of the Argentine Armed Forces. It became the standard rifle and over 150,000 were delivered in a number of variations. Nearly 122,000 of these were constructed by FMAP under licence. This particular example is one of the Para versions with 21 inch barrel and a folding stock.

In addition to 7.62 mm, a 5.56 mm calibre variant has been developed to reduce costs and enable the soldier to carry more ammunition and this gives better control of automatic fire. It was referred to as the Carbine Automatique Leger (CAL) but proved unsatisfactory. However, the principal of the design continued and resulted in the FNC.

The FAL has also been used by Brazil, Cambodia, Chile, Ecuador, Germany, Indonesia, Ireland, Israel, Kuwait, Libya, Luxemburg, Netherlands, Paraguay, Peru, Portugal, Qatar, Santo Domingo, South Africa, Syria and Venezuela.

TYPE:	**7 MM/.280 IN FAL ASSAULT RIFLE**
MANUFACTURER:	Fabrique Nationale d'Armes d G Herstal (FN)
DATE IN USE:	1950
COUNTRY OF MANUFACTURE:	Belgium
OPERATION:	gas, selective fire
FEED:	20 round magazine
LENGTH:	40.1 in/1,018 mm
WEIGHT:	9 lb/4.09 kg
EFFECTIVE RANGE:	328 yd/300 m (sights to 656 yd/600 m)

A 7 mm/.280 in calibre development of the Fusil Automatique Leger (FAL) or Light Automatic Rifle was entered by the UK as a contender in the 1950 light rifle trials together with the EM2. This rifle was subsequently adopted as the replacement for the No 4 rifle but in the new standard NATO 7.62 mm calibre as the L1A1.

TYPE:	**7.92 MM HAKIM (DOCTOR) RIFLE (AG42)**
MANUFACTURER:	Maadi
DATE IN USE:	1950
COUNTRY OF MANUFACTURE:	Egypt (Sweden)
OPERATION:	gas, semi-automatic
FEED:	10 round magazine
LENGTH:	47.13 in/1,197 mm
WEIGHT:	9.6 lb/4.36 kg
EFFECTIVE RANGE:	875 yd/800 m (sights 109 yd/100 m to 1,094 yd/1,000 m)

The AG42 is the Swedish Armed Forces version of the 6.5 mm Ljungman semi-automatic rifle that was adopted in 1942. It was eventually replaced by a modified NATO G3 in Swedish service from 1965.

Illustrated is the Hakim which is an Egyptian manufactured version of the AG42, built by Maadi. During the early 1950s, Swedish technicians helped set up a small arms manufacturing plant in Egypt. The Hakim is the 6.5 mm AG42 which has been modified to 7.92 mm and is fitted with a full length hand guard, a revised sight, muzzle brake and a modified magazine clip.

A 4.5 mm air rifle and a .22 in variant have also been built for training purposes.

TYPE:	**9 MM PM SELF-LOADING PISTOL**
MANUFACTURER:	Makarov
DATE IN USE:	1950
COUNTRY OF MANUFACTURE:	USSR
OPERATION:	blowback, self-loading, double-action
FEED:	8 round magazine
LENGTH:	6.25 in/159 mm
WEIGHT:	1.7 lb/0.77 kg
EFFECTIVE RANGE:	close quarters

The 9 mm Makarov is similar in appearance to the Walther PP. It was designed to give the best performance with an unlocked breech. It is generally well made although the handling is slightly awkward due to the style of grip.

The 9 mm Makarov is the standard pistol of the former Soviet and Warsaw Pact Countries such as East Germany (Pistole M), and it was also made available to some countries that received Soviet military aid.

TYPE:	**7.62 MM VZ52 RIFLE**
MANUFACTURER:	State factories
DATE IN USE:	1952
COUNTRY OF MANUFACTURE:	Czechoslovakia
OPERATION:	gas, semi-automatic fire only
FEED:	10 round magazine
LENGTH:	39.1 in/993 mm
WEIGHT:	8.25 lb/3.75 kg
EFFECTIVE RANGE:	close quarters (sights 109 yd/100 m to 984 yd/900 m)

The Czech Model 52 would appear to combine a number of existing design features such as the gas system of the MKb.42 and the M1 trigger, together with a few original features. However, in 1952 – the date of its introduction – this would hardly be classed as an advanced rifle. In addition it uses a longer 7.62 mm cartridge than the standard Russian 7.62 mm.

This particular VZ52 was captured from the Egyptians during Suez Operations.

TYPE:	**7.62 MM TYPE 56 ASSAULT RIFLE**
MANUFACTURER:	State factories
DATE IN USE:	1956
COUNTRY OF MANUFACTURE:	China
OPERATION:	gas, selective fire
FEED:	30 round magazine
LENGTH:	33.9 in/861 mm
WEIGHT:	8.13 lb/3.69 kg
EFFECTIVE RANGE:	306 yd/280 m (sights to 800 yd/875 m)

Although given the same designation as the carbine on page 66, this Chinese Type 56 assault rifle is a copy of the Soviet AK-47. At least two variants of this weapon exist – the original has a removable knife bayonet, while this later production model has a folding cruciform section bayonet attached to the bottom of the front sight base. The Type 56-1 is fitted with a folding metal stock, while the 56-2 has a sideways folding butt/stock.

TYPE:	**7.62 MM L1A1 SLR RIFLE**
MANUFACTURER:	Royal Small Arms Factory (RSAF)/BSA
DATE IN USE:	1957
COUNTRY OF MANUFACTURE:	UK
OPERATION:	gas, semi-automatic fire only
FEED:	20 round magazine
LENGTH:	44.2 in/1,123 mm
WEIGHT:	9.75 lb/4.43 kg
EFFECTIVE RANGE:	328 yd/300 m (sights to 200 yd/183 m and 600 yd/549 m)

The L1A1 is the British version of the FN FAL (built to imperial measurements). This rifle was a long time coming for the British services, as the SMLE family of bolt action rifles had proved to be very reliable and the authorities wanted to be sure that they were getting a real improvement. The L1A1 replaced the No.4 Mark I rifle within the British Army and remained the standard rifle until the adoption of the SA80.

Licence production of the L1A1/FAL has been carried out in Australia as the L1A1, L1A1 F1 (shortened version) and L2A1 automatic weapon with heavy barrel. It has also been built in Canada and India, and used by Barbados, Gambia, Guyana, Malaysia, New Zealand, Oman and Singapore.

TYPE:	**7.62 MM M14 RIFLE**
MANUFACTURER:	Harrington & Richardson Arms Co
DATE IN USE:	1957
COUNTRY OF MANUFACTURE:	USA
OPERATION:	gas, selective fire
FEED:	20 round magazine
LENGTH:	43.75 in/1,111 mm
WEIGHT:	9.25 lb/4.20 kg
EFFECTIVE RANGE:	820 yd/750 m (sights 109 yd/100 m to 1,000 yd/914 m)

The M14 is descended from the M1 Garand but much work was expended in eliminating faults with the previous rifle. As a result, following completion of Light Rifle trials, it became the standard rifle of the US Army with production conducted by Harrington & Richardson, Thompson Products (TRW), Winchester and Springfield. The M14 is capable of firing in semi and automatic mode, but most M14s have their selectors locked in the semi-automatic mode. This reduces the amount of ammunition expended and encourages the soldier to take proper aim, thus making the rifle more effective.

It was adopted by USA on completion of Light Rifle trials for which it was designated T44.

Variations on the M14 include two versions of folding stock. The M14A1 was developed for the squad automatic weapon and is fitted with a bipod. Fire can be selected to automatic as well as semi-automatic.

TYPE:	**9 MM MODEL 59 PISTOL**
MANUFACTURER:	Norinco
DATE IN USE:	1959
COUNTRY OF MANUFACTURE:	China (USSR)
OPERATION:	blowback, self-loading, double-action
FEED:	8 round magazine
LENGTH:	6.25 in/158 mm
WEIGHT:	1.75 lb/0.79 kg
EFFECTIVE RANGE:	close quarters

This is a Chinese copy of the Soviet 9 mm Makarov. It is functional but crudely finished in places as well as being slightly heavier.

TYPE:	**7.62 MM AKM ASSAULT RIFLE**
MANUFACTURER:	State Factories
DATE IN USE:	1959
COUNTRY OF MANUFACTURE:	USSR
OPERATION:	gas, selective fire
FEED:	30 round magazine
LENGTH:	34.5 in/876 mm
WEIGHT:	6.94 lb/3.15 kg
EFFECTIVE RANGE:	328 yd/300 m (sights to 1,094 yd/1,000 m)

The AKM is an updated and slightly lightened version of the AK-47 with muzzle chambered to reduce climb when fired on fully automatic. It has been supplied to Egypt and Syria as well as the former Warsaw Pact countries. In addition the AKM and variants have been built in Germany (MPi KM), Iraq (Tabuk), Hungary (AKM- 63 and AMD-65), Poland (PMKM) and Romania.
A variant of the AKM is the AKMS which has a metal folding stock. This is of a stamped steel construction while the AKM is made from laminated wood.

Variants of the AKM have been been built in Germany, Hungary, Poland and Romania as well as the former Soviet Union. It has been used by most countries of the former Warsaw Pact as well as numerous other countries. This particular example came from Zimbabwe.

TYPE:	**7.62 MM G3 ASSAULT RIFLE**
MANUFACTURER:	Heckler & Koch
DATE IN USE:	1959
COUNTRY OF MANUFACTURE:	Germany
OPERATION:	delayed blowback, selective fire
FEED:	20 round magazine
LENGTH:	39.8 in/1,011 mm
WEIGHT:	10.5 lb/4.77 kg
EFFECTIVE RANGE:	1,094 yd/1,000 m (sights 109 yd/100 m to 437 yd/400 m)

The G3 is the current rifle of the German Army and although it fires the full 7.62 mm round, many of its design characteristics are carried forward from the MP44, StG45 and CETME assault rifles. For training purposes the bolt can be replaced and the G3 can fire plastic ammunition. Alternatively, a specially designed tube can be fitted together with bolt and magazine enabling the use of 5.56 mm/.223 in ammunition.

Heckler & Koch have built several variants. The G3 A3 is the standard rifle with a plastic stock and handguard, the G3 A3ZF is the same weapon but fitted with a telescopic sight and the G3 A4 has the plastic stock replaced by a retractable version.

The G3 has been built under licence in Greece, Norway, Portugal, Sweden (AK4) and Turkey.

TYPE:	**9 MM HELWAN (MODEL 1951)**
MANUFACTURER:	Danshway
DATE IN USE:	1960
COUNTRY OF MANUFACTURE:	Egypt (Italy)
OPERATION:	short recoil, self-loading, single-action
FEED:	8 round magazine
LENGTH:	7.88 in/200 mm
WEIGHT:	2.12 lb/0.97 kg
EFFECTIVE RANGE:	close quarters

The Beretta Model 1951 was developed for the Italian armed forces. It was adopted by Israel and Nigeria and a licensed copy was manufactured in Egypt by Danshway as the Helwan during the early 1960s

The Model 1951 later led to the Beretta Model 92.

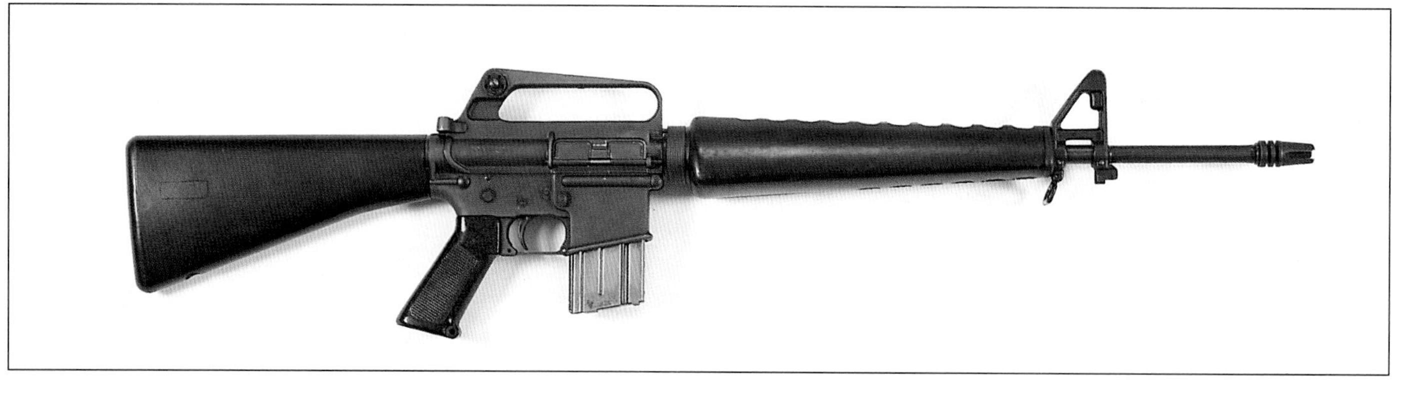

TYPE:	.223 IN AR-15/M16 RIFLE
MANUFACTURER:	Colt
DATE IN USE:	1961
COUNTRY OF MANUFACTURE:	USA
OPERATION:	gas, direct action, selective fire
FEED:	20 and 30 round magazine
LENGTH:	38.25 in/972 mm
WEIGHT:	6.25 lb/2.84 kg
EFFECTIVE RANGE:	219 yd/200 m (sights to 500 yd/458 m)

The AR-15 was designed by Eugene Stoner who was an employee of Armalite Inc. It was designated M16 upon adoption for military use and various models have been built over the years.

The M16 is a lightweight, low impulse rifle, firing a lightweight bullet at high velocity. In its M16A2 form it is capable of being operated in semi-automatic, three shot burst or fully automatic mode. The M16A1 and M16A2 models of the M16 became the standard rifle of the US forces.

A development of the M16 is the Colt Industries ACR. This weapon was designed to meet the US Army requirement for an Advanced Combat Rifle (ACR). The Colt ACR proposal is an improved M16A2 providing a better muzzle brake/compensator which helps reduce the recoil effect and reduced barrel climb. It is understood that in the competition against other weapons by Steyr-Mannlicher, Heckler & Koch and AAI, the margin of improvement was insufficient to warrant proceeding further and the project went into abeyance.

The M16 Assault rifle is used by over 50 countries worldwide and in excess of 8,000,000 examples have been built.

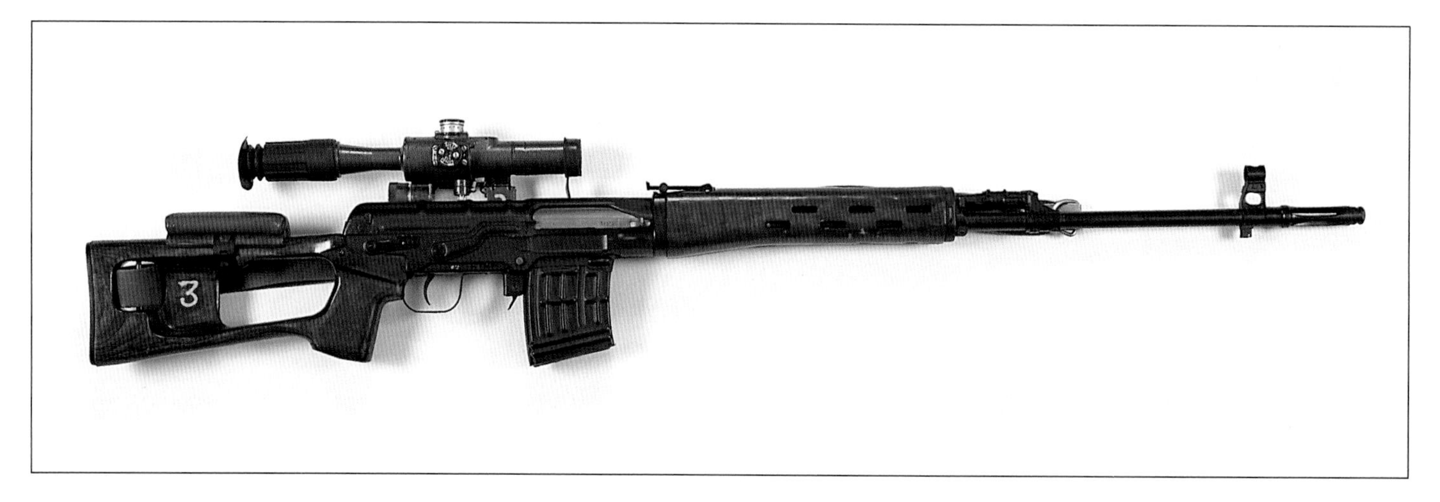

TYPE:	7.62 MM DRAGUNOV SVD SNIPER RIFLE
MANUFACTURER:	State Factories
DATE IN USE:	1963
COUNTRY OF MANUFACTURE:	USSR
OPERATION:	gas, short-stroke piston, semi-automatic
FEED:	10 round magazine
LENGTH:	47.3 in/1,201 mm
WEIGHT:	9.51 lb/4.32 kg
EFFECTIVE RANGE:	875 yd/800 m

The SVD (Self Loading Rifle) or Dragunov replaced the M1891/30 sniper rifle in Soviet service. It is fitted with a 4x Model PSO-1 telescope, and a range finder scale which is graduated to the height of a man to assist in the estimation of the range. It uses a similar action to the rest of the AK series and has a sizeable cut-out to the butt to reduce weight. The Dragunov is used by most of the former Warsaw Pact countries.

TYPE:	**7.62 MM L42A1 RIFLE**
MANUFACTURER:	RSAF (Enfield)
DATE IN USE:	1969
COUNTRY OF MANUFACTURE:	UK
OPERATION:	manual, single shot
FEED:	10 round magazine
LENGTH:	46 in/1,168 mm
WEIGHT:	13 lb/5.90 kg
EFFECTIVE RANGE:	820 yd/750 m (sights optical)

The L42A1 is a conversion of the World War Two .303 in No.4 Mark I(T) or Mark I*(T) rifle to take NATO 7.62 mm ammunition and is used as an improved sniper rifle.

This particular rifle was built as a No.4 Mk.I(T) in 1944 before being converted to L42A1. It is fitted with an L1A1 sight and retains the original wooden cheek piece from the original sniper rifle. The British Army replaced the L42A1 with the L96A1.

TYPE:	**5.56 MM AR70 ASSAULT RIFLE**
MANUFACTURER:	Beretta
DATE IN USE:	1970
COUNTRY OF MANUFACTURE:	Italy
OPERATION:	gas, selective fire
FEED:	30 round magazine
LENGTH:	37.1 in/942 mm
WEIGHT:	8.75 lb/3.97 kg
EFFECTIVE RANGE:	437 yd/400 m (sights 164 yd/150 m to 328 yd/300 m)

The AR70 was the result of Pietro Beretta's survey and evaluation of existing 5.56 mm rifles. His design incorporated the forward locking, two-lug bolt system of the Soviet AKM and the M1 Garand.

The AR70 is used by the Italian Special Forces, Jordan and Malaysia.

Variants of the Model 70 (AR70) include the SC with folding stock and LM light machine gun with a bipod and carrying handle. The rigid stock of the AR70 can easily be replaced by the folding one used on the SC70.

TYPE:	**5.56 MM FAMAS ASSAULT RIFLE**
MANUFACTURER:	GIAT (St Etienne Arsenal)
DATE IN USE:	1972
COUNTRY OF MANUFACTURE:	France
OPERATION:	delayed blowback, selective fire
FEED:	25 round magazine
LENGTH:	29.8 in/757 mm
WEIGHT:	8.25 lb/3.75 kg
EFFECTIVE RANGE:	437 yd/400 m

The Saint Etienne FAMAS was designed to fire the 5.56 mm M193 round and have the firepower of an assault rifle together with the ease of use of a sub-machine gun. The result was this bullpup design for the French Army. It has a single, three shot burst and fully automatic firing capability.

GIAT solved the problem of spent cases in bullpup rifles by fitting the FAMAS with a two position extractor – left or right ejection. It is also fitted with a spring buffer to reduce the recoil impact on the firer's shoulder.

Several versions of the FAMAS have been developed, including the Export, which is intended for the overseas commercial market. This has only a single shot capability and cannot be used for grenade launching. The FAMAS Civil has a 570 mm barrel compared to the standard 488 mm and is calibred to take the .222 Remington. This rifle was intended for the French commercial market and like the Export model, was incapable of burst or automatic fire or of firing grenades. A FAMAS Commando variant has also been built for commando or special forces use. This rifle has a 405 mm barrel and no grenade launching capability, otherwise it is identical to the standard FAMAS.

The FAMAS is used by the French Army as well as Djibouti, Gabon, Senegal and the United Arab Emirates.

TYPE:	**5.56 MM MODEL 372 GALIL ARM ASSAULT RIFLE**
MANUFACTURER:	IMI
DATE IN USE:	1972
COUNTRY OF MANUFACTURE:	Israel
OPERATION:	gas, selective fire
FEED:	12, 35 and 50 round magazine
LENGTH:	38.13 in/968 mm
WEIGHT:	10.13 lb/4.60 kg
EFFECTIVE RANGE:	437 yd/400 m

The Galil was designed as a multi-purpose weapon, assault rifle, light support weapon and sub-machine gun. Further variants include the AR which has a folding stock, no bipod or carrying handle. The Short Assault Rifle or SAR is similar to the AR but fitted with a shortened stock. In addition, a 7.62 mm sniping rifle variant has been built which is capable of placing shots inside a 12 to 15 cm circle at 300 m range and a 30 cm circle at 600 m range.

For those models fitted with a bipod, this serves two purposes as it also incorporates a highly effective barbed wire cutter. In many respects the design and mechanism are modelled on the AK-47 series.

The Galil replaced the FN FAL in Israeli service from 1973.

TYPE:	**5.45 MM AKS-74 ASSAULT RIFLE**
MANUFACTURER:	State arsenals
DATE IN USE:	1974
COUNTRY OF MANUFACTURE:	Romania (Russia)
OPERATION:	gas, selective fire
FEED:	30 round magazine
LENGTH:	36.6 in/930 mm (28.9 in/734 mm folded)
WEIGHT:	8.25 lb/3.75 kg
EFFECTIVE RANGE:	328 yd/300 mm (sights to 1.094 yd/1,000 m)

The AKS-74 has the folding butt which is the more common form of the AK-74. Further variants are the RPK-74 machine gun and AKSU-74 sub-machine gun.

This Romanian version is also capable of single fire and three round burst and is fitted with a forward pistol grip.

TYPE:	**5.56 MM FNC ASSAULT RIFLE**
MANUFACTURER:	Fabrique Nationale Herstal
DATE IN USE:	1975
COUNTRY OF MANUFACTURE:	Belgium
OPERATION:	gas, selective fire with 3 round burst controller
FEED:	30 round magazine
LENGTH:	39.25 in/997 mm
WEIGHT:	8.38 lb/3.8 kg
EFFECTIVE RANGE:	437 yd/400 m (sights to 273 yd/250 m and 437 yd/400 m)

The FNC resulted from a requirement for a 5.56 mm calibre FAL which was simple in all aspects: simple to manufacture, simple to use and simple to disassemble and reassemble in the field. The original and the subsequent CAL designs, based on the FAL, were unsuccessful. A fresh design led to the FNC and it entered production in 1980. It still did not meet with the success of the original 7.62 mm FAL.

Two variants of the FNC are available – the standard and a short barrelled version. It has a folding light alloy butt stock and a fixed plastic stock.

It is used by the armed forces of Belgium, Indonesia, Nigeria, Sweden, Tonga and Zaire.

TYPE:	**9 MM MODEL .92FS SELF-LOADING PISTOL**
MANUFACTURER:	Pietro Beretta
DATE IN USE:	1976
COUNTRY OF MANUFACTURE:	Italy
OPERATION:	short recoil, semi-automatic with single or double-action
FEED:	15 round magazine
LENGTH:	8.25 in/210 mm
WEIGHT:	2.25 lb/1.02 kg
EFFECTIVE RANGE:	close quarters

The 9 mm Beretta Model 92FS is part of the Model 92 family of semi-automatic pistols which entered production in 1976. It is of similar design and appearance to the previous Models 81 and 84, but the Model 92 is larger and more powerful and has the blowback replaced with short recoil.

The Model 92FS is similar to the rest of the family except that it has a modified trigger-guard and extended base to the magazine to suit a two-handed grip, curved front edge to the grip frame, new grip plates and lanyard ring. The barrel has been chromed internally and external surfaces have been coated in 'Bruniton' which is a Teflon-like material.

The Model 92FS was selected in 1990 as the US Forces replacement for the Colt 1911. The Model 92 family is used by Brazilian, Italian, and some other armed forces as well as various police forces.

TYPE:	**7.62 MM SIG SG542 ASSAULT RIFLE**
MANUFACTURER:	Sphinx
DATE IN USE:	1977
COUNTRY OF MANUFACTURE:	Switzerland
OPERATION:	gas, selective fire
FEED:	20 or 30 round magazine
LENGTH:	38.9 in/1,000 mm (29.13 in/751 mm folded)
WEIGHT:	7.75 lb/3.52 kg
EFFECTIVE RANGE:	875 yd/800 m (sights 109 yd/100 m to 656 yd/600 m)

The SG542 is part of the 540 series of SIG assault rifles. While the SG540 and 543 are chambered for 5.56 mm ammunition, the SG542 is chambered for 7.62 mm. They are all built to the same basic design and have a number of parts in common. The SG542 can be fired as a single shot, three round burst or fully automatic. The trigger guard can be rotated to enable a mittened hand to operate the trigger in Arctic conditions.

The SG542 has been licence built in France, Portugal and Chile and has also served in Bolivia, Burkina Faso, Chad, Djibouti, Ecuador, Gabon, Indonesia, Ivory Coast, Lebanon, Mauritius, Nicaragua, Nigeria, Oman, Paraguay, Senegal, Seychelles and Swaziland.

TYPE:	**7.62 MM MODEL VZ58P ASSAULT RIFLE**
MANUFACTURER:	Uhersky Brod
DATE IN USE:	1977
COUNTRY OF MANUFACTURE:	Czechoslovakia
OPERATION:	gas, selective fire
FEED:	30 round magazine
LENGTH:	32.75 in/844 mm
WEIGHT:	6.13 lb/2.80 kg
EFFECTIVE RANGE:	437 yd/400 m (sights 109 yd/100 m to 875 yd/800 m)

The indigenous Czechoslovak Model 58 bears more than a passing resemblance to the AK-47. The stock is made from plastic impregnated wood fibre.

Variants of the Model 58 include the folding metal stock 58V and the 58Pi with a bracket for night sight. The 58Pi is also usually fitted with a light bipod and an enlarged conical flash suppressor.

The Model 58 is used by the former Soviet armed forces and some Warsaw Pact armed forces.

TYPE:	**4.85 MM XL65E5 INDIVIDUAL WEAPON**
MANUFACTURER:	BSA
DATE IN USE:	1977
COUNTRY OF MANUFACTURE:	UK
OPERATION:	gas, single shot and automatic burst
FEED:	20 or 30 round magazine
LENGTH:	30.5 in/775 mm
WEIGHT:	8.50 lb/3.86 kg
EFFECTIVE RANGE:	437 yd/400 m (sights optical)

The Individual Weapon (IW) is a small calibre bullpup design which was selected by the British and entered for the NATO small arms trials. It was fitted with the SUSAT (Sight Unit Small Arms Trulux). It was designed at the same time as the Light Support Weapon (LSW) with which parts were 80% common. Although this proved to be an excellent weapon, unfortunately for the British, .223 in/5.56 mm calibre was deemed by NATO to be the ultimate projectile for future standardisation.

TYPE:	**9 MM VP70M AUTOMATIC PISTOL**
MANUFACTURER:	Heckler & Koch
DATE IN USE:	1977
COUNTRY OF MANUFACTURE:	Germany
OPERATION:	blowback, semi-automatic and selective fire, double-action
FEED:	18 round magazine
LENGTH:	8 in/203 mm (21 in/533 mm with stock)
WEIGHT:	2.13 lb/0.97 kg
EFFECTIVE RANGE:	close quarters

The VP70 is of unusual design with just four operating parts. Considerable use of plastics is made in its construction and the manufacturers claim that it has a life of 30,000 rounds.

The VP70M (Military) can be fitted with a holster, and also a stock which, when fitted, activates a toggle lever and permits the firin of three round bursts. The burst is at a rate of 2,200 rounds per minute. Consequently a large magazine is fitted.

A variant is the VP70Z (Zivil) which is for the civil market and therefore does not have the burst capability.

TYPE:	**5.56 MM STEYR ARMEE UNIVERSAL GEWEHR AUG/A1**
MANUFACTURER:	Steyr-Daimler-Puch
DATE IN USE:	1978
COUNTRY OF MANUFACTURE:	Austria
OPERATION:	gas, selective fire
FEED:	30 and 42 round magazine
LENGTH:	31.1 in/790 mm with 20 in/508 mm barrel
WEIGHT:	8.5 lb/3.86 kg with 20 in/508 mm barrel
EFFECTIVE RANGE:	328 yd/300 m (sights optical)

The Armee Universal Gewehr or AUG is a bullpup design by Steyr which is capable of utilising any one of four different barrels. The 350 mm is for a sub-machine gun variant, 407 mm as a carbine, 508 mm as a rifle and 621 mm as an automatic weapon.

This assault rifle version of the AUG which is illustrated, has a translucent plastic 30 round magazine. The heavy barrelled automatic variant is fitted with a bipod and 42 round magazine. It can be converted in seconds to a carbine or LSW. With upper receiver and RARDE rail attached, the AUG is compatible with the British SUSAT sights. The bipod includes an integral wire cutter.

The AUG is in service with the Irish, Moroccan, Omani and Saudi Arabian armed forces. It is also licence built for the Australian and New Zealand armed forces as the F88. A semi-automatic variant is available for police forces.

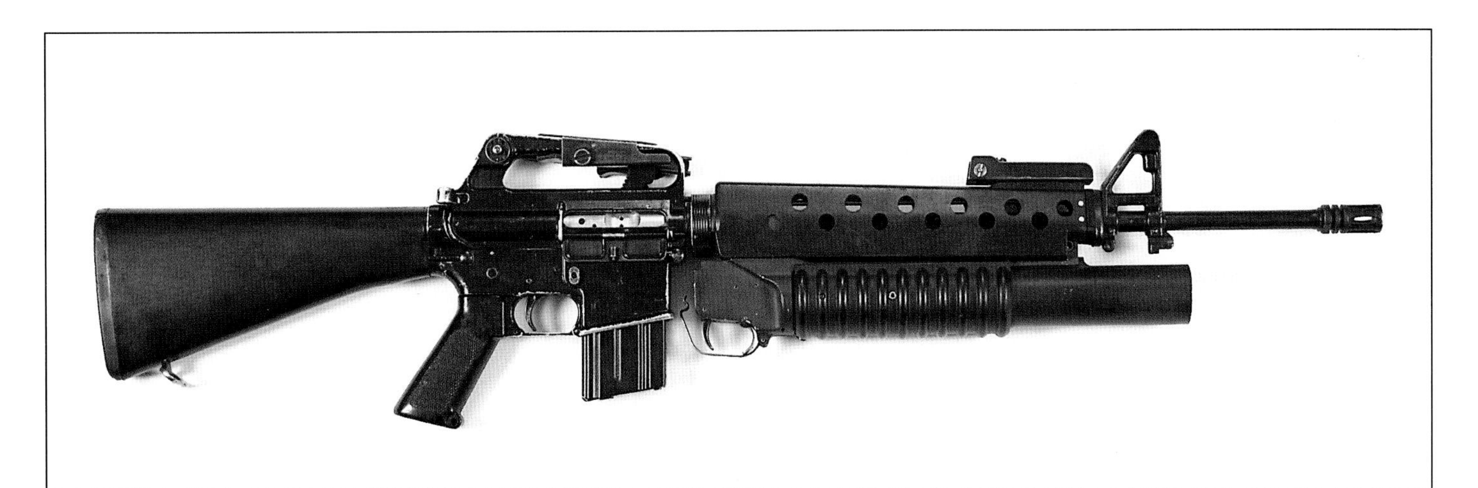

TYPE:	**.223 IN AR-15/M16 ASSAULT RIFLE + M203**
MANUFACTURER:	Colt
DATE IN USE:	1980
COUNTRY OF MANUFACTURE:	USA
OPERATION:	gas, selective Fire
FEED:	20 or 30 round magazine
LENGTH:	27.75 in/705 mm
WEIGHT:	5.2 lb/2.36 kg
EFFECTIVE RANGE:	219 yd/200 m (sights 100 yd/91 m to 500 yd/457 m)

This M16 is fitted with the 40 mm M203 grenade launcher which was designed by AAI in the late 1960s but, apart from initial production, all were manufactured by Colt. The M203 is issued as an independent attachment to the M4 as well as the M16A1 and M16A2 rifles. It has also been built in Austria by Steyr for their AUG family of rifles. In the USA, an improved version designated M203PI has been built which can be fitted to most rifles/assault rifles.

TYPE:	**.223 IN (MODEL 733) COMMANDO ASSAULT RIFLE**
MANUFACTURER:	Colt
DATE IN USE:	1980

The Model 733 Commando assault rifle is a compact version of the M1A2 which has been designed to provide a robust weapon which enables quicker action. The Commando assault rifle can be carried and used much as a sub-machine gun and provides instant, accurate fire. It may be used in a variety of tactical roles including non-infantry units. The Commando assault rifle was used by the Special Forces during the Vietnam War.

TYPE:	**5.56 MM AC556 RIFLE**
MANUFACTURER:	Sturm, Ruger & Co Ltd
DATE IN USE:	1980
COUNTRY OF MANUFACTURE:	USA
OPERATION:	gas, self loading, selective fire
FEED:	5, 20 or 30 round magazine
LENGTH:	38.4 in/975 mm
WEIGHT:	7.3 lb/3.31 kg
EFFECTIVE RANGE:	437 yd/400 m

The Ruger AC556 selective fire weapon is similar in appearance to the Ruger 5.56 mm Mini-14/20GB infantry rifle, which, in turn, is an adaptation of the standard Mini-14 commercial and military rifle. The AC556 differs from the Mini-14 series in that it is fitted with a three position selector lever fire control mechanism. The positions for this lever provide semi-automatic, three shot burst and fully automatic fire.

TYPE:	**7.62 MM M82 SNIPER RIFLE**
MANUFACTURER:	Parker-Hale
DATE IN USE:	1980
COUNTRY OF MANUFACTURE:	UK
OPERATION:	bolt, single shot
FEED:	4 round magazine
LENGTH:	44.9 in/1,140 mm
WEIGHT:	14 lb/6.36 kg
EFFECTIVE RANGE:	437 yd/400 m

Parker-Hale have manufactured a family of sniper rifles based on the Mauser 98 action. The M82 series of sniper rifles is part of this family. It is a precision weapon which has been optimised to provide a 99% chance of hitting a target first time out to 437 yd (400 m).

A further development from the M82 is the L81A1 Cadet Training Rifle. This M82 sniper rifle has been fitted with an L8A1 Weapon Sight Image Intensifier for night operations instead of normal Pecar V2S telescopic sight.

TYPE:	**5.56 MM STERLING ASSAULT RIFLE 80**
MANUFACTURER:	Chartered Industries
DATE IN USE:	1980
COUNTRY OF MANUFACTURE:	Singapore
OPERATION:	gas (piston, short stroke), selective fire
FEED:	20 or 30 round magazine
LENGTH:	37.7 in/967 mm
WEIGHT:	7.2 lb/3.25 kg
EFFECTIVE RANGE:	437 yd/400 m

The SAR 80 was designed by Frank Waters in 1976 and production commenced in 1980 for the Singapore armed forces. Some 45% of components are sheet metal pressings while a further 40% are commercially available standard parts which keep production costs down. A folding butt/stock variant is also available.

TYPE: **9 MM P.225 (SIG) PISTOL**
MANUFACTURER: Sauer
DATE IN USE: 1981
COUNTRY OF MANUFACTURE: Switzerland
OPERATION: recoil, single or double-action
FEED: 8 round magazine
LENGTH: 7 in/180 mm
WEIGHT: 1.8 lb/815 g
EFFECTIVE RANGE: close quarters

The P.225 (or P.6) is similar in design to the P.220 but is smaller and lighter. This pistol does not have a safety catch and results in a very fast first shot – comparable with a revolver. Should the situation require it, weapon safety on the P.225 enables a round to be loaded into the chamber and held there in readiness. The cocked hammer can be lowered by pressing down on the hammer de-cocking lever which is located slightly behind and on the left of the trigger. The result is that the firing pin is locked by a pin which stops any movement, even when dropped.

The P.225 can be fired either double-action by squeezing the trigger its full range or single-action whereby the hammer is cocked by hand and only a tight pressure is required on the trigger.

A training version of the P.225, the P.255PT, has been designed to fire a plastic bullet.

TYPE:	**5.56 MM G.41 RIFLE**
MANUFACTURER:	Heckler & Koch
DATE IN USE:	1982–83
COUNTRY OF MANUFACTURE:	Germany
OPERATION:	roller lock, delayed blowback
FEED:	20 or 30 round magazine
LENGTH:	38.7 in/993 m
WEIGHT:	9.5 lb/4.33 kg
EFFECTIVE RANGE:	875 yd/800 m

The 5.56 mm G41 was developed from the HK33 which was a scaled-down 5.56 mm variant of the successful G3. This was developed following lessons learned from the NATO small calibre trials. It has a single shot, three shot and fully automatic fire capability. Amongst the features included in the rifle are low noise and it is fitted with a positive action bolt closing device and a bolt catch which keeps the bolt open when the magazine is empty, facilitating a quick return to fire on loading a fresh magazine.

A number of variants include the short barrel G41K and the G41A2, both of which are fitted with retracting stocks.

TYPE:	**9 MM GLOCK 17 SELF-LOADING PISTOL**
MANUFACTURER:	Glock
DATE IN USE:	1983
COUNTRY OF MANUFACTURE:	Austria
OPERATION:	short recoil, self-loading
FEED:	18 round magazine
LENGTH:	8 in/203 mm
WEIGHT:	1.56 lb/0.71 kg
EFFECTIVE RANGE:	close quarters

The 9 mm Glock 17 was developed to meet an Austrian Army requirement for a new pistol. It is manufactured from a combination of steel and plastic parts.

The Glock 17 is a locked-breech, short recoil, self-loading pistol. It has no conventional safety catch but will only fire if the trigger is correctly pulled.

Three variants of the Glock 17 have been produced. The standard Glock 17, the Glock 17 Amphibious and the Glock 17L. The standard Glock 17 can be converted to a fully amphibious version with a slight modification. The 17L is the same design as the standard with a longer barrel and slide. A development of the Glock 17 is the Model 18 which has a selective fire three round burst capability.

The Glock 17 family is in service in NATO armed forces, and special forces as well as police departments of many countries.

TYPE:	**5.45 MM AK-74 ASSAULT RIFLE**
MANUFACTURER:	State arsenals
DATE IN USE:	1984
COUNTRY OF MANUFACTURE:	USSR/CIS
OPERATION:	gas, selective fire
FEED:	30 round magazine
LENGTH:	36.25 in/921 mm (27 in/686 mm folded)
WEIGHT:	7.5 lb/3.41 kg
EFFECTIVE RANGE:	328 yd/300 m (sights to 1,094 yd/1,000 m)

The 5.45 calibre is now standard issue to CIS forces and its use has spread to other former communist block countries to the extent that it is rapidly replacing the Kalashnikov AK-47 and AKMs. It is easily identified from its predecessors by a horizontal groove on the butt.

This is essentially a modernised AK-47/AKM design with barrel, bolt and magazine built to take new calibre ammunition. It is fitted with a muzzle brake which is intended to enable the firer to engage a target with a burst without the line of fire being moved off the subject. In many weapons the second and third round would be high. The result is that, as well as all rounds landing where aimed, the recoil is reduced. A disadvantage of this system is that the design of the muzzle brake is such that the excessive deflected gases and noise have become very dangerous to anybody within a few metres either side of the firer.

It is used by the former Soviet armed forces and some Warsaw Pact armed forces.

TYPE:	**.5 IN LIGHT FIFTY MODEL 82A1 SNIPING RIFLE**
MANUFACTURER:	Barrett
DATE IN USE:	1984
COUNTRY OF MANUFACTURE:	USA
OPERATION:	short recoil, semi-automatic
FEED:	10 round magazine
LENGTH:	56 in/1,440 mm
WEIGHT:	34 lb/15.55 kg
EFFECTIVE RANGE:	1,096 yd/1,000 m

The Barrett 'Light Fifty' Model 82A1 sniping rifle has been designed to be used for long-range interdiction as well as sniping. It can also be used as a defensive weapon for ocean-going light craft. It is fitted with a x10 telescope which is calibrated from 547 yd (500 m) to 1,968 yd (1,800 m) which is considered to be the maximum range when using standard Browning machine gun ammunition.

The Model 82A1 is used by the US Air Force, US Army, US Marine Corps – EOD and Special Forces.

TYPE:	**7.62 MM TABUK ASSAULT RIFLE (AKM)**
MANUFACTURER:	State Arsenal
DATE IN USE:	1985
COUNTRY OF MANUFACTURE:	Iraq (USSR)
OPERATION:	gas, selective fire
FEED:	30 round magazine
LENGTH:	40 in/1,016 mm
WEIGHT:	9.13 lb/4.15 kg
EFFECTIVE RANGE:	328 yd/300 m (sights to 1,094 yd/1,000m)

The Tabuk is a copy of the Kalashnikov AKM. This example is chambered to fire the 7.62 mm cartridge and is fitted with an integral grenade launcher and sight.

Variants of the AKM have been built in East Germany, North Korea (Type 68), Romania and Yugoslavia.

TYPE:	**5.56 MM L85A1 INDIVIDUAL WEAPON (IW) SA80 WITH SUSAT**
MANUFACTURER:	Royal Ordnance (Enfield)
DATE IN USE:	1985
COUNTRY OF MANUFACTURE:	UK
OPERATION:	gas, selective fire
FEED:	30 round magazine
LENGTH:	30.5 in/775 mm
WEIGHT:	10 lb/4.54 kg
EFFECTIVE RANGE:	437 yd/400 m

The British Army has been experimenting with new small calibre rifles for front line troops since World War Two. The L85A1 was the eventual product and has been adopted as the rifle for the British Armed Forces. It was developed from the XL65E5 Individual Weapon (IW) and is constructed from a range of pressed and dropped steel together with high impact nylon. It is a conventional weapon with rotating bolt which engages in lugs behind the breech and carried in a machined carrier which runs on two guide rods while a third rod controls the return spring. The L85A1 Individual Weapon (IW) is one half of the Enfield Weapon System, the other being the L86A1 Light Support Weapon (LSW). The L85A1 has replaced the L1A1 in the British Services.

The L85A1 is fitted with the SUSAT (Sight Unit Small Arms Trilux) L9A1 x4 sight that was developed by RARDE. The L98A1 is a manually operated cadet version of the L85A1 without the gas actuating system. This rifle has a rear sight/carrying handle and can be fitted with a .22 barrel for training purposes.

TYPE:	**9 MM MODEL 93R AUTOMATIC PISTOL**
MANUFACTURER:	Pietro Beretta
DATE IN USE:	1987
COUNTRY OF MANUFACTURE:	Italy
OPERATION:	short recoil, single shot or 3 round burst
FEED:	15 or 20 round magazine
LENGTH:	9.75 in/268 mm (22.1 in/561 mm with stock)
WEIGHT:	3.09 lb/1.40 kg (2.56 lb/1.16 kg with stock)
EFFECTIVE RANGE:	close quarters

The Model 93R is an advanced self-loading pistol capable of single or three round burst. This pistol has a forehand grip fitted to the front of the trigger-guard which can be folded down. This provides a better hold for the second hand, rather than clasping the butt with two hands when firing at a difficult or long range target. When firing in the burst mode the Model 93R must be held with both hands. It is also recommended that, if time is available, a folding stock is fitted.

TYPE:	**.38 IN MODEL 64 STAINLESS REVOLVER**
MANUFACTURER:	Smith & Wesson
DATE IN USE:	1989
COUNTRY OF MANUFACTURE:	USA
OPERATION:	double-action
FEED:	6 shot cylinder
LENGTH:	6.75 in/171 mm (2 in/50 mm barrel)
WEIGHT:	1.75 lb/0.79 kg
EFFECTIVE RANGE:	close quarters

The Model 10 has proved to be a popular revolver with military and police forces. This satin finish, stainless steel variant has advantages for military use due to its resistance to corrosion. This example has the 2 in (50 mm) barrel while a 4 in (101 mm) barrel is also available.

TYPE:	**7.62 MM L96A1 SNIPER RIFLE**
MANUFACTURER:	Accuracy International
DATE IN USE:	1990
COUNTRY OF MANUFACTURE:	UK
OPERATION:	bolt action
FEED:	10 round magazine
LENGTH:	44 in/1,118 mm
WEIGHT:	14.3 lb/6.49 kg
EFFECTIVE RANGE:	656 yd/600 m

The 7.62 mm PM was designed from the outset as a sniper rifle. While it is fitted with iron sights, it is normal for the PM or L96A1 as the British Army designated it, to have the Schmidt und Bender L1A1 6 x 42 telescopic sight fitted. During trials, the British Army required a first round hit at 656 yd (600 m) and accurate harassing fire out to 1,094 yd (1,000 m) which was easily achieved by this rifle. As well as the British Army, the PM is used by several African, Far East and Middle East countries.

INDEX